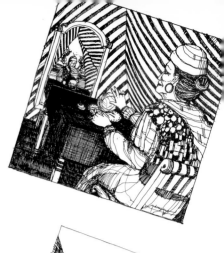

WHAT? ANOTHER NORTHWOODS READER?

Written by Cully Gage
Illustrated by Andrew Amor
Cover Photo by Hoyt L. Avery

Copyright 1987
by Cully Gage
and
Avery Color Studios
AuTrain MI 49806

Library of Congress Card #87-71381
ISBN 0-932212-51-4

First Edition—June 1987
Reprinted—1988, 1990, 1992

Published by Avery Color Studios
AuTrain, Michigan 49806

Printed in Michigan, U.S.A. by
Lake Superior Press
Marquette, Michigan 49855

TABLE OF CONTENTS
AND ILLUSTRATION LISTING

"Now we build fire, eh? Goodbye winter! Goodbye cold. Here come spring."

I was watching her very carefully as she read my valentine greeting, then turned the big heart over to see the tiny "C" I'd written down at its point.

Just before the man stoked the fire for the night and went to bed the mouse was eating barley out of his hand.

So the Swede soaked half a package of Peerless Smoking tobacco in a big pail of water, made a little broom of chicken feathers, and brushed the leaves with the brown liquid.

and the two old ladies were feeling the wine when Tante Cherie proposed that Madame Olga read her own fortune in the crystal ball.

We shared everything. If we went to pick wild strawberries or flowers for our mothers, we made sure that neither of us had a bigger handful.

It infuriated her to see him sleeping so deeply and happily while filling the bedroom with bedlam. Her wedding night! And thousands more to go!

Alas, he slipped and fell into the big pool below the bridge but not until I heard him shout, still in mid-air and before the splash, "Enjoy! Enjoy!"

Old Blue Balls was enraged. No one had ever challenged his authority before. He put his face close to the father's and roared,

After what seemed like an eternity of torture, the barber swung the chair around so I could see his handiwork. The hair was short, all right.

Emerging from the kitchen a moment later with a cake of Fels Naphtha soap in one hand and a wet washcloth in the other, she bade me stick out my tongue which she anointed.

FOREWORD

Yes, another Northwoods Reader. I had thought to end my anecdotage by entitling its immediate predecessor *The Last Northwoods Reader* but my memories of the people I knew as a boy in the Upper Peninsula of Michigan are like the water of a forest spring: the more that flows out, the more comes in. I've had so many fine letters from my readers asking for another batch of tales that I could not resist the temptation to reminisce again. Besides, old men (I'm now 81) enjoy reliving their past so forgive me.

Cully Gage

If you would enjoy writing Cully:
Cully Gage
3821 W. Milham
Portage, MI 49002

THE MAN WHO KILLED WINTER

John Kangas was worried about his wife Lena. It wasn't just that she'd stopped talking and spent the days sitting in the rocking chair with an unread bible in her lap. No, it was that she no longer kept the house neat and the food she put on the table was poorly prepared. How long had it been since she did a real washing to hang on the lines in the living room off the kitchen? "Aren't you feeling good, Lena?" he'd asked her. "Maybe you should go see Dr. Gage, eh?" "No, I'm all right," she said with a sigh and she sighed often these wintry days. For the first time John noticed that Lena was looking old.

It's cabin fever, John thought. Lena had a right to feel depressed. Lord, this had been the worst winter of their lives. The first snow that had come in October was still there under the four or five feet of more snow that had covered it. Now it was the second week in March with little hope of spring because another great storm had swept down from Lake Superior building new big drifts and when it stopped a deep cold had settled in. Twenty, thirty below for days on end. For the first time in memory Silverthorn and Company had shut down their logging operations north of town because the horses and oxen, belly deep in the snow, couldn't skid out the logs and it was just too cold for man or beast. No one went outside unless they really had to. There was none of the usual visiting back and forth between neighbors for conversation and coffee. After you'd slogged your way to the outhouse and back you had to sit on a stool and plant your feet on the open door of the kitchen range for ten minutes before the cold began to leave your bones. Yes, it was a rough time.

Lena wasn't the only one in Tioga who was depressed. The whole town was in the dumps. My father, the doctor, said he'd never had so many calls from people who weren't really sick though they thought they were. "Sometimes I think they just want to see another human face, housebound as they are," he told my mother. "Of course I always give them a bottle of my special tonic which is half grain alcohol, strong enough to set their gullets afire. I tell them to take a teaspoonful every four hours. The old women especially swear by that tonic. Doesn't hurt 'em; just makes them feel better. All they really need is a thaw and to have the crows come back." When Father Hassel, our Catholic priest, came up for his weekly chess game, glass of whiskey and a cigar, he made the same diagnosis. "Their souls are snow-sick, Doctor. Only four people showed up for mass last Sunday."

One of the few people in our town who wasn't depressed was John Kangas. People called him the Happy Finn and he always seemed to be that way whatever the weather. A big man with a big laugh, he made you feel good just to be around him. Always smiling, always joking, he often did zany things like the time on Midsummer's Day when he painted some crooked-neck gourds to look like penguins and put them up in his front yard when the temperature hit ninety.

John did his utmost to cheer his wife but his little jokes just turned her face to the wall. "Ah, Lena, it's March. Spring come. Sisu!" (Sisu is that lovely Finnish word that has no English equivalent. Roughly translated, it means enduring and coping gallantly. No matter what, you can triumph over any adversity. That word is why the Russians were never able to conquer Finland.)

But Lena wasn't having any sisu and John couldn't give it to her. She just sighed another long sigh. "Sounds like the suds going down the kitchen sink," John thought and grinned. If only they'd been able to have children all would be well. It was a deep sorrow between them. Perhaps he could get her a little puppy or a kitten. No, this wasn't puppy season and Lena had never liked cats. John went to the store and bought a pail of new coffee, a can of peaches, and some candy. That didn't help at all. He went down to the basement, sprouted all the potatoes, and even peeled a pot full of them so she wouldn't have to but Lena didn't even say thanks.

A bit discouraged, John shoveled a wide path through the big drift on the way to the outhouse, digging out three parallel trenches so they'd fill up first if it began to blow again. Lena didn't use the path, just used the slop jar. To make her comfortable, he banked snow around the house foundations to keep out the drafts, and he got up at midnight to put more wood in the kitchen stove, then got up again early to do it again so it would be warm when she arose. Lena didn't seem to notice.

Something had to be done. He'd go and get Dr. Gage to come see Lena. Maybe he'd give her some strong medicine. Suddenly, as John was putting on his boots, an idea hit him so hard it almost bowled him over. He'd make Lena smile. Yes, he'd make the whole town laugh. No more being down in the dumps. When he told Lena what he was going to do she said, "Oh Yonnie, you going crazy too now" but she smiled and patted his cheek. Whee! Full of exhileration, John could hardly wait to begin.

But first he had to take down the stove pipe from the old pot bellied stove in the summer kitchen. John looked it over. Once that stove had heated their living room until the grates burned out because of too hot fires from anthracite coal. Then they had moved it into the summer kitchen to heat extra washing water but they'd only used it once. Lena had been after him for years to get it out of the house so she could have more room. Well now he'd kill two partridges with one stone.

Taking down stovepipes is always a dirty job. Even if you tap them first to shake down the soot always there'll be a cloud of it when you take off that first section. Lena appeared with an armfull of potato sacks from the cellar. At least she was out of that damned rocking chair, John thought. As she spread the sacks around the stove, Lena asked, "You not going move stove by yourself, Johnny?" "No," he replied, "I go get Okkari." He sure felt good now that Lena was talking again.

Okkari, his next door neighbor and good friend, was happy to have an excuse to get out of the house. "Yah, Johnny. I help. We use my big sledge with ski runners to take stove behind barn or where you want it."

By the time they returned Lena already had the stovepipes down, the cap in the chimney hole, and was shaking out the potato sacks by the back door. "First time for months she'd been out of the house," John thought. Cold as it was, a bit of fresh air would do her good. With a lot of grunting the two men finally got the big stove onto the sledge.

"Where we haul it? Back of barn?" Okkari asked.

"No we put stove in front of house, over there on little hill next to street."

"Why you put stove there, Johnny?"

John told him his wonderful wild idea as he was to tell many others later. "Too damned cold too long. I going kill winter. I going heat all outdoors. I keep fire going till spring come."

It took time for that to sink in before Okkari began to laugh and laugh and laugh. They kept laughing so hard they could hardly pull the sledge. Even through the walls, Lena heard them, pressed her face against the pane and they saw her laughing too.

After much effort the two men finally got the sledge up the little hill and then had to shovel a lot of snow before they hit solid ground. Taking an elbow off the stove pipe they erected a nine foot length of pipe straight up so they'd get a good draft.

"Now we build big fire, eh? Goodbye winter. Goodbye cold. Here come spring!" John went after birchbark and kindling and Okkari went to his house to get small wood and kindling, he said. When he returned, still laughing he held out a bottle of whiskey. "Here your kerosene, Johnny," he said, and they took turns tipping it until a column of white smoke rose up into the winter sky.

Entering the house, John was sure feeling good and he felt even better when he saw that a smiling Lena had cooked venison and mashed potatoes. Before they went to bed she insisted on putting some more wood in the stove outside. It was twenty three below zero.

The next morning John had pancakes with thin fried slices of salt pork just the way he liked it. "Get the fire going, Yonnie," Lena ordered. "There's no smoke coming out of the pipe." Then she giggled. Oh how John liked to hear

11

that giggle. "Look, Yonnie. It's working. Thermometer says only nineteen below." It was the first time in a month it had been that warm.

So John built a new fire and had it going good by the time old man Marchand, our mail carrier, passed by, bringing up the morning mail pouch from the railroad station. "Whoa, Maude, whoa!" he commanded his old horse. Winding the reins around the whip, he came up to see what was going on. "For why you make fire in ze stove way out here?" he asked. When John told him the old man burst into laughter. "Ah, mon ami," he said. "I like zat. Ze winter, she's going to go now." He shook John's hand hard before he climbed back on his sleigh.

Okkari came next, then Reino, then some others. All of them had to put wood in the stove. "We make it through the winter now," one said as he tried to warm his hands. He almost had to touch the stove itself before he felt any real warmth. The men didn't care. They were warmed by their laughter.

That afternoon many others appeared to keep the fire going, so many that Okkari brought over some boards to serve as benches. When they got too cold, John invited them in for coffee and yakking. Lena didn't mind a bit.

The news of John Kangas' challenge to the gods of winter spread like wildfire through our forest village of Tioga. Somehow it twanged a universal chord: Make it through the winter. Make spring come. No more cold in the bones.

It's probably hard for people from Down Below to understand the deep hunger of our people to escape their yearly hibernation. John's gesture galvanized every soul in the village. They climbed our hill street to see his hot stove in the snow. They laughed themselves out of their gloom. Heat the whole outdoors! The notion was just so outrageous it was almost believable. Even if it weren't, it didn't matter. Just to get out of the dumps and laugh again was enough.

Lena had never before had so many visitors, nor had to make so much coffee. All her women friends and even others she didn't know so well came to see, to put a bit of wood in the stove, and to talk with her. Best of all were the children. Coming home from school, they milled around her front yard squealing, playing fox and geese. When one little girl, cold and shivering, knocked at the door to ask for a glass of water and to get warm, Lena melted, gave her a hug and a cookie too. It was a mistake. Soon many other kids were coming in and calling her "*aiti*(mother) Lena" and begging for cookies. Sometimes she even had to shoo them out so she could whip up another batch but it was so good to see happy little children in her home.

That night the fire never went out in the stove. Of course John had stoked it good before he went to bed but Charley Olafson, our constable and night watchman, filled it up again after making his midnight rounds, and Okkari, having to take a pee about three in the morning replenished it again. Then someone, no one knew who, put enough new wood in the stove so that it was burning fiercely when John arose next morning. Altar fires must not go out.

That day the gifts came in. Pierre LaPoint brought up a load of dry maple poles on his logging sleigh behind the team, then helped John shovel out a place by the stove to put them. Reino Erickson brought two armloads of pine boards and split them for kindling. Okkari hauled over a sawbuck and bucksaw and every man who came sawed up some of the maple. Little chunks about eight inches long seemed to burn better. Soon there was quite a stack, enough so that everyone could have a piece to put on the fire.

Lena got plenty too. Mrs. Saarinen came with cinnamon rolls; Mrs. Oyalla with saffron bread and a tub of new churned butter; Mrs. Mattson with a plate of that delicious Finnish soft cheese that looks like custard pie. Several others brought big bags of korpua, that dry cinnamon toast for coffee slurping. All brought gaiety.

That afternoon Father Hassel stopped in on his way back from making a pastoral visit to Bridget Murphy and the beloved pig that she kept in the kitchen because it was too cold in the shed. Smiling, he too put a piece of wood in the stove and when he left, he said to John, "Bless you, my son. You have acquired merit," and the next Sunday he preached a sermon on the need to be joyous unto the Lord. "You have let winter defeat you, my children," he said. Then he told them about John Kangas and urged them to bring a stick of joy to put in his stove.

That sermon brought more French Canadians up our long hill street than ever before. You could almost feel the whole village coming together, all old animosities forgotten. Some even brought bottles of home-made wine: pincherry, chokecherry or wild raspberry. A festival it was. Lena invited them all in for coffee. For many of those French Canadians it was the first time they'd ever been in a Finlander's house.

Knowing the drain, someone brought up a huge five gallon coffee pot and five pounds of coffee along with four chipped lumber camp mugs to be used by anyone and soon the big pot was steaming on the stove. Someone else brought a box of Domino sugar lumps. When Arvo Mattila proposed that he'd bring over a big kettle of venison stew, John said no. Enough was enough! The joke was getting out of hand. Too many people coming. It wasn't John's stove any longer. It was Tioga's.

Then the Marquette Mining Journal sent a reporter up on the train to interview John and Lena and take pictures. When it published a big article on the second page of the next edition, John and Lena were famous. Annie, the postmistress, posted the whole page on the bulletin board. More people came to see and take pictures too. Too much! John began to wish that he'd never gotten that crazy idea. What to do? He'd let the fire go out but our people kept it going despite his wishes.

I don't know what might have happened but the problem solved itself. A great thaw occurred. The sun shone; the great snowbanks melted into rivers that ran down the street. The crows came back. There was joy in Tioga beyond measuring. An early spring, thanks to John Kangas and all the people of our town who had put sticks in the stove. We once again had made it through the winter.

VALENTINE'S DAY

Happy ♡ Valentine's Day

distribute

deposit

In the Upper Peninsula of Michigan, the U.P., February is the cruelest month. The wind roars down from the Arctic bringing one big snow after another. The pale sun has no warmth in it, not even enough to melt the hoarfrost on the windows. Yet, in our little forest village of Tioga there was one week in February that was full of gaiety and anticipation, the week before Valentine's Day.

Of course Valentine's Day wasn't as good as Christmas or the Fourth of July but it came close, perhaps because it came at half past winter. Flynn's Store always had a fine display of valentines on the front counter which we kids ogled but rarely bought. Only big people bought them to express their affections or their hatreds. Hatreds? Yes, some of the cards were terribly insulting. On the outside there might be a heart or flower but when you opened it up you'd see a picture of some old hag or devil with a bit of nasty sentiment. I remember one that said "Roses are red and violets are blue; I'm not so hard up I have to love you!" And another whose verse read: "I tell you true; I'm on the level; I hate your guts; Go to the Devil!" Oh there were a lot of them like that which found their way into the post-office boxes over which Annie Anderson presided. She said she never could understand why Old Blue Balls, our tough school superintendent, got so many valentines until she peeked in one that was unsealed and read the insults within.

14

But most of the valentines on the rack were nice ones, full of expressions of affection, pictures of pink cupids shooting yellow arrows into red hearts. Lots of pictures of flowers; lots of mush! Most of them cost five cents but there were some that cost a quarter. These had a lot of paper lace on them. And there was one that cost a dollar which had been in the valentine rack for many years. A bit soiled it was from the many hands that had opened it to see the accordion display of fifty little hearts, each containing the worlds "I love you." They say that Pete Ramos finally bought it one day when he was drunk, not because he had someone to give it to but just because it was so pretty. They say that someone who visited him one evening a year later found the old man opening and reopening that valentine by the light of his kerosene lamp and mumbling "I love you", words that he had probably never heard from the lips of a woman.

We kids never bought any of Flynn's store valentines; we made our own. Early in the week before Valentine's Day, our beloved teacher, Miss Feeley, had shown us how to make hearts by folding a sheet of paper in half, then with the school's snub-nosed scissors cutting the outline of half a heart on the outside edge of the fold. When unfolded, there was a perfect heart, a miracle. Fisheye, my friend, was so entranced he swiped one of those scissors and spent two hours in his outhouse making hearts of different sizes out of the Ladies Underwear section of the Sears Roebuck catalog.

I spent the week before The Day making some valentines. The first was for my mother. My attempt wasn't very good, mainly because I had only the stub of a red crayola to use in coloring the paper so I put the mess in the kitchen stove and looked for something already red. In the pantry I found an empty box of chocolates that was really scarlet so I asked mother if I could have it. When she said it was all right I traced a heart on it and began to try to cut it out but it was too hard so again when I asked for help, mother did it for me. I did cut out a smaller heart and pasted it in the middle of the larger one and printed on it these words:

> " *Roses are red and violets are blue*
> *I try to be good but sometimes I'm bad*
> *And that makes you sad*
> *But I love you.*"

I wasn't very happy with the result. Too smeary. I'd put too much water in the flour to make the paste.

Then I made another smaller valentine for my little sister, Dorothy. She didn't get any poem - just a smiling face inside a traced heart - but she couldn't read yet anyway. That was enough work for one day, and time to get the paste out of my hair.

With only two days left before the big day, I began my major opus, a valentine for Amy Erickson, whom I had long adored secretly and from afar. Amy was a lovely little Swede girl with blonde curls I wanted to stick my fingers into. She was smart too, the only other person in my grade who made all A's like I did, but it was her up-tilted nose and wild giggle that really attracted me. Not that she knew it nor did anyone else, for I was very, very shy. Indeed I don't think she had ever looked at me or spoken to me.

For some time I'd been dreaming of a valentine for Amy that would make her notice me. I'd make the biggest valentine in the whole world, I would. Yes, I'd get some baling wire and shape it into a heart ten feet tall and cover it with cedar and ground pine and hang a red ribbon at the notch saying "Amy, be my valentine, yours, Cully Gage" and then I'd put it up against our classroom door so all the kids would have to step through it to enter. But we didn't have that much baling wire and the ground pine lay buried under six feet of snow and collecting all that cedar from the swamp would take a week. No, that wouldn't work; I'd have to think of something else. All I knew was that Amy's valentine had to be a big one, bigger than others she might get.

After some thought an inspiration hit me. Up in the attic were some remnants of wall paper rolls from which I might be able to cut out a huge heart. Galloping up the stairs I found a dandy. It was blue mainly but covered with bright red roses. Using part of it to fold and cut a pattern, then tracing the huge heart on another piece, I had a valentine that must have been two feet across. This I pasted on a big sheet of cardboard to get the curl out. In its center I had another smaller heart of white paper on which I printed "Amy, please be my Valentine," but then I lost my nerve. I just couldn't write "From Cully." I could just see Fisheye and Mullu and all the other kids snickering. Finally, I just printed the letter "C" very small on the back side of the heart near its point. Maybe Amy would know I'd made it for her. Then I contrived a huge envelope for the valentine out of butcher's paper that my mother used to wrap packages and wrote Amy's name on the front of it.

I got to school very early on Valentine's Day to find that Miss Feeley already had the big valentine box on her table. It was a lovely thing, all covered with white tissue paper and red hearts. In its middle was a large slot into which the valentines were to be put but of course the slot wasn't big enough for mine so I just put it under the box, tingling with excitement, as I went out to play till the bell rang.

When it did ring and the room filled with kids waving their valentines, Miss Feeley called us sternly to order. "Here on the table is your Valentine box. Beginning with the first row, you will march up here and deposit (She then wrote the word 'deposit' on the blackboard) your valentines in the slot. We will then forget about them until after recess when we'll open the box and distribute (She spelled the word 'distribute' for us and wrote it on the board too) the valentines to each of you. Now let's forget about the box until after recess." Well, I hadn't expected that ! My valentine to Amy was already up there under the box. My friend Mullu had told me on the playground that he hadn't made any damned mushy valentine for any damned girl or anyone else so I watched what he did when it was his turn. Mullu just marched up there scowling and pretended to drop something in the slot, so when I had to march up I pretended too. The sharp eyes of the other kids noticed of course and Mullu and I had to put on the macho act when teased at recess. Leo Belill overdid the teasing and I had to poke him a good one in the nose before he quit.

Finally it was time to open the box. "Now children, come to order. We'll do this efficiently and calmly. Each of you in turn will come to the box, reach in, pick up a valentine, read the name on it, and then bring it back to that person. There is no need to read the name aloud."

As she turned to the box she saw my big valentine to Amy under it. "Oh, here's one that was too big to fit in the box," she said. "It's for you, Amy, so come up and get it before the others take turns." Amy squealed with delight and tore the envelope off it before she got back to her seat, then waved it for all of us to see. "It's the biggest valentine I ever got," she said with that wild giggle of hers.

As you can imagine, I was watching her very carefully as she read my valentine greeting, then turned the big heart over to see the tiny "C" I'd written down at its point. "Oh, it's from you, Carl. Oh thank you, thank you," she said as she turned to a boy, Carl Failla, who sat next to her. And she held his hand a long time. The dirty bugger didn't deny it and I almost died.

No one noticed my reaction. Then each of us, in turn, marched up to the valentine box, reached in, and delivered a valentine to the person to whom it was addressed and trying to read it on the way. The one I grabbed was for Mullu. It was a "You-know-who", a "From you know who.." We all knew who. It was from Miss Feeley, our teacher, who always stuffed the box with valentine hearts for the children she thought wouldn't get any. All the "You-know-whos" were alike, just simple red hearts like the ones on the valentine box, and all saying, "Be my valentine."

Fisheye and Mullu got you-know-whos and some of the kids got a lot of valentines. I got none! I slumped down in my seat trying to hide my stricken face. Nobody noticed.

No one except Miss Feeley who came down and put her hand on my shoulder. "Didn't you get a valentine, Cully?" she asked. "Oh, I'm so sorry." "Yeah, I got one," I replied and pulled it out of my pocket to show her. It was a red heart with a bit of paper lace from the shelf paper in our kitchen pantry, and it said, "Be my valentine, Cully. From Amy."

ERICK NIEMI AND THE KANGAROO MOUSE

When I was a boy in the U.P. we had three kinds of mice, woods mice, house mice and kangaroo mice. Actually I think the woods mice and the house mice were the same species. Certainly they looked alike as they scampered across our floors. Every autumn some woods mice came into our houses to spend the winter with their house mouse cousins or they would hide in the hay and straw stacks. Rarely did they get completely out of control. Most of our families had cats and mouse traps and if all else failed Pete Half Shoes would let you put Mabel, his pet skunk and bedpartner, down in your cellar for a small fee. Nothing better than a skunk to catch mice.

The third variety, the kangaroo mice, were much more rare. Seldom did we find them in our houses; they preferred our hunting cabins in the forest. I've only seen three of them in my whole life and that occurred when I spent a week alone up at our old hunting cabin just after Christmas one year.

My father who knew everything about everything said that their real name was jumping mice, not kangaroo mice, that the Latin term for them was *mus zapus.* Most mice can jump but the house and woods mice jump horizontally; kangaroo mice also jump vertically. They sit up on their haunches like a squirrel with their long tails behind them, then crouch down and leap straight up in the air, then do it again and again just for the hell of it. Maybe that's why some of our folk called them dancing mice. Oh, they don't always jump; usually they scamper like other mice when they are going some place. They seem to reserve their leaping for exhibition purposes, for jumping with joy.

But they also can jump horizontally if they have to. One of those I saw up at our old hunting cabin leaped from the corner of our table to the bench that holds our water pail, a distance of six feet. The furthest I could ever jump from a standing position was four feet and that kangaroo mouse did it sitting down. Of course I don't have a fat little tail to give me a boost. That tail, by the way, has a white tip while that of other mice does not.

Usually jumping mice hibernate the winter away except if they live in a warm cabin with plenty of crumbs. In the wild they subsist on an underground fungus, Dad said, called Endogone, which gives them both food and water but inside a cabin they'll eat anything any mouse would eat - which is everything.

I've had to tell you all this so you can understand what Erick Niemi had to tackle in order to tame and make a pet of a kangaroo mouse. Erick was one of Tioga's two hermits. The other one was old man Coon who had a gold mine up on the headwaters of the Tioga River. I've written about him and the three jugs of gold he had hidden in his spring in my first *Northwoods Reader* so I won't tell about him here except to say that he only came to town twice a year. Erick Niemi was different. He came to town twelve times a year, on the first of each month, to pick up his little pension check at the post office and buy his necessaries. Unlike Old Man Coon, Erick was always friendly. In the summers when some of us kids went to his little cabin by Horseshoe Lake at the edge of a huge cedar swamp, he was glad to see us, glad to have the company, and glad to have some of the little trout we caught in the shallow creek that ran through the swamp. We enjoyed seeing him cook them. First, he scraped the slime off with his hands, then he'd squeeze them. "Always squeeze them till they squeak" he'd say, then put them in a pan and fry them crisp brown. Never cleaned them. All the brook trout in that creek were small ones, six inches long or less and Erick ate them bones and all, head first, with some hardtack and tea or water for a chaser. Mullu and I tried them and they were very good. Sometimes we'd haul a pail of water for him from the spring at the edge of the hill near his little potato patch. No, Erick wasn't the kind of hermit who hates people. He just preferred living in that little cabin in the swamp. He didn't need people but enjoyed them when they came his way. Not many did because his shack was two miles from town and a half mile from Horseshoe Lake. Erick had been a miner and had a little pension which, with rabbits, deer, partridge, fish and potatoes, provided what he needed. He loved his swamp and the quiet, he said, and was never really lonely except sometimes in the long winter.

Erick's cabin was well made, though very small. So was its door; you bowed to enter. Inside, it was rather dark despite two little windows, one behind the small table, and the other behind the bench which held two water pails. On the west end Erick had his narrow bunk fastened to the wall and with its own roof of boards, the space above being a catch-all for tools, baskets, skis, snowshoes, oh, a lot of things. Nails on the logs held an assortment of clothing, blankets and cloths. Most unusual was Erick's stove. It was almost three feet square and two feet high. Fine both for cooking and warming. Erick said it had come from an old abandoned lumber camp.

Above the stove, suspended from the ceiling, was a long pole on which wet socks and other stuff hung. The only furniture was an old rocking chair with a seat of potato sack filled with grass, and an empty nail keg. Oh yes, there was also a table next to the south window with a dirty plate, cup, bowl and utensils. On the wall behind the table was one of M.C. Flynn's calendars with many of the days crossed out. Erick explained that he crossed them so he'd know when he had to go to town for the mail. He had no clock or watch, just ate and slept when he wanted to do so. But all in all, the little cabin was fairly clean and on the table was a bean can with some fresh cedar in it. It was snug, and I guess that was the best you could say for it.

Outside the cabin there wasn't much to see except the swamp. Erick had a woodshed on the west side of the cabin that was filled one third with small wood and two thirds with chunks to keep the fire going overnight. Some kindling and birch bark filled one corner. Not too far from it was Erick's crapper consisting simply of a skinned log between two trees and a closed box holding a Sears Roebuck catalog. If it was awful cold at night, Erick said, rather than put on his boots, he just peed in an old Peerless tobacco pail and heaved it out the next morning. A simple life but it was good enough for Erick Niemi.

People wondered how Erick kept busy spending his days and nights in the swamp. "I don't have to keep busy," he answered. "That's the best part of it." Often in the winter he had a project or two. One winter he cleared and blazed trails all through the swamp so he could have easier walking. This particular year of 1915 he'd been making a snowshoe because the old left one was in such bad shape. Just held together with baling wire mainly. Anyway, making a snowshoe from scratch takes a bit of doing. Because he had cut them from a young ash tree the summer before he had the strips for the frame, and he also had the rawhide for the webbing. Boiling the woodstrips until they were supple enough to be curved around a snow-shoe shaped path made of nails on a board wasn't too hard but it was patient work. Even more time consuming was making the holes for the rawhide with an old hand drill someone had given him. Since the bit wasn't the right size Erick had to burn out each hole with a nail heated in the stove until it was big enough to thread the rawhide through. Then he had to soak that rawhide and make pegs to hold it tight until he could make a new part of the webbing.

Just making a handle for his burning nail took a whole day. First he had to cut a length from a slender maple sapling, cut out a V-shaped groove to hold the nail, cut a little horizontal notch to hold the nail head, and replace the strip. To hold the nail tight, Erick cut a strip of tin from a pork and bean can, bound it around the handle and tacked it in place. It worked fine but holding the outfit in the coals burned his hands so he had to contrive a tin shield out of the can. That worked perfectly so he called it a day.

Erick never hurried. He didn't know what hurry was. He walked slowly, moved slowly, and talked slowly even when he was talking to himself. Rarely did he work at anything longer than a half hour at a time. Always there was something else to do —if he wanted to do it. He could get a pail of water from the spring, or wander his trails in the swamp, or trim the wick of his kerosene lamp or lantern, or fill the woodbox, or grease his boots. Usually he just smoked his old corncob pipe until he felt the urge to go back to his snowshoe. He ate when he was hungry and went to bed when it was dark, if he wanted to. Not such a bad way to live.

But when the snowshoe was finished about the middle of January Erick found himself getting restless. Why he even went to town in the middle of the month, took coffee with the Pesolas and had a long sauna. After one sniff Mrs. Pesola offered to wash and iron his long underwear while he was in the sauna and he let her do it, then had more coffee and toast before he took the trail home. Why, she had even given him a new pair of socks. The new snowshoe worked fine.

Yet Erick still was restless. What he needed was another long time project for the rest of the winter. That evening it came to him in the shape of a little mouse. He was sitting in his rocking chair smoking his corncob pipe and watching the flames from the open door of the stove flicker on the logs when a mouse poked its head through the knothole in one of the boards of the cabin floor, came through it and began to dance in the firelight. Erick had never seen anything like it. The mouse would sit on its hindquarters looking around the room then suddenly take off in a series of leaps, sit down, then jump again. Finally, when Erick coughed, it made a long leap and disappeared down the knothole.

"I got company," Erick said to himself and the idea came to him that he'd spend the rest of the winter taming that crazy little critter. Climbing into his bunk he went to sleep trying to figure how to do it.

In the morning he remembered that this was soup day or rather soup week so he spent the time using his hacksaw to cut off a piece of bone from the hindquarter of venison that hung frozen in the woodshed. Putting this in his big cast iron pot along with some slices of salt pork, potatoes, an onion and a collection of rabbit and partridge bones, he dumped in part of a box of barley to thicken it. Barley? Hey the mouse might really go for that.

The cabin was too bright in the morning for mice because the sun came in through the windows on the south and east but by three o'clock in the afternoon it was really dusky, almost dark, almost time for his jumping mouse to appear. Realizing that he'd need to know what the mouse preferred to eat, Erick placed three little piles of food not far from the hole, the first of barley, the second of korpua crumbs, and the third of mashed hazelnut meats. Then, opening the door of the stove, Erick sat in his chair waiting.

It took only two pipes of tobacco before the kangaroo mouse popped out of the knothole. This time, however, it didn't jump or go for the food. Instead it scurried like any other mouse all along the base logs of the cabin, exploring, it seemed. It even entered an old boot before disappearing into its hole. Erick was disappointed. He spent some time trying to figure out an appropriate name for him. "Nikki," he said at last, "I'll call him Nikki." That made Erick grin because there was a man in our town, Nicholas Oland, whom we called Nikki and who really looked like a mouse with his receding chin, sloping forehead, big nose and large ears that stuck out from his head. Yes, Nikki Kangaroo it would be.

"Tulla Nikki," (Come, Nikki) Erick called softly and probably just by chance the mouse came out of his knothole. "A Finn mouse," Erick thought. "Already he understands Finnish." This time the mouse was hungry and it sniffed, then sampled each of the three tiny piles of food in turn. It ate several small bits of the smashed hazelnuts and, finding one whole nut among them, held it in his little paws and gnawed it round and round until it was gone. "Just like beavers," thought Erick. "They have to keep their teeth sharp." Nikki only ate a few crumbs of the korpua toast before trying the barley. That he loved. Made him squeak and dance. When it was devoured Nikki spurned the other food and disappeared down the knothole.

About every half hour that evening Nikki came back for more barley, Erick putting only five grains of it on the floor each time and moving the barley a little closer to his feet. Just before the man stoked the fire for the night and went to bed the mouse was eating barley off his boot. And the next night out of his hand by the boot. And the next evening Nikki allowed himself to be picked up and fondled as he ate out of Erick's hand.

I won't go into all the other details of the taming but soon Erick had a good little friend and companion. Often he'd come when called, run up Erick's leg and into the side pocket where the old hermit kept a few handfuls of barley. He never invaded Erick's bunk though and when Erick tucked him in his pocket to get wood or roam his trails Nikki just stayed there munching until they returned. Good company. Erick talked to him a lot and the old man was very content.

Then danger suddenly invaded Erick's little cabin. He'd been making the rounds of the trails in the swamp, had caught a mink by the creek and had snared a snowshoe rabbit. Nikki wasn't in his pocket this time; Nikki was a late sleeper. Rarely did he appear before three in the afternoon. By the time Erick had skinned the mink and rabbit, fleshed the mink skin, tacked it to the woodshed wall, and dressed the rabbit it was time for soup and a chunk of hardtack. Afterwards he was sitting in his chair enjoying his pipe when suddenly out of the knothole Nikki ran, squeaking in terror to climb up his leg and bury himself in the old man's pocket. What the devil had got into the mouse? Soon he understood. A white sloping head appeared at the knothole, a weasel emerged, sniffed around a second or two, followed Nikki's trail scent up to Erick's foot, then began to climb his leg. Erick roared and brushed it off, tried to hit it with his stub of a broom, and finally the weasel went back down the knothole.

Few people nowdays know much about weasels, the most bloodthirsty animals on earth. Only about ten inches long, brown in summer and white in winter, they are absolutely fearless. And tenacious! Once on the trail of prey, they keep following it until finally they spring, clamp their long sharp teeth usually in the carotid artery behind the ear and suck blood until the victim expires. They feed on things much bigger than they are — rabbits, chickens, birds, and they especially like mice. They are killers, often killing many more than they need. Erick knew that Nikki didn't have a chance down there below the cabin floor so he emptied out an old cigar box full of things like scissors, needles and thread, bored air holes in the top of the box, lined it with an old sock and some barley, and after putting Nikki in it, tacked it shut. Now that the mouse was safe, Erick deliberated for some time where to put the box. At first he thought of putting it in his bunk but somehow he didn't fancy having a weasel prowling around his naked sleeping throat so he put it on the table instead. Daytimes he let Nikki out after plugging the knothole or he carried the mouse with him in his pocket as he roamed his swamp trails.

Weasels seldom stay in the same place long. They're roamers and so Erick hoped that this one would soon leave. But the bugger hung around day after day and night after night. Often when he'd poke his white head out of the knothole Erick would try to hit it with the stove poker but never came close. He tried to snare it with a little loop of picture wire surrounding the hole. Didn't work. He thought of suspending a large chunk of wood over the hole with a fishline over a nail that he could let go when the varmint appeared but decided instead to try to shoot it with his 22 calibre rifle. Erick hated to do it. Too much noise in his cabin! Too close quarters and the bugger, even when he emerged from the knothole, was always moving. Finally, after three misses, Erick got him. Not in the head but in the body and he had to club it with the poker before it finally succumbed.

I wish I could say that Erick and Nikki lived happily ever after but unfortunately one night a terrible windstorm tore through the swamp. Never had Erick heard the wind roar like that or so many trees going down. The next morning all his swamp trails were a tangle of windfalls. "Well, there's another year's project," Erick thought as he started out to see if he'd gotten any rabbits in his snares. Since the trails were hard packed because he had snow-shoed them so often he just walked them in his boots. Just before he got to the place where he had put his first snare Erick was confronted by a huge windfall. Three big spruce trees had come down in the storm right across the path. Then the old hermit broke one of the unwritten laws of the woods: Never climb over anything you can walk around. Breaking off several of the stubby fir branches, Erick tried to make his way through the tangle but he slipped and fell hard. As he did so he heard or felt something crack in his right leg before a flood of excruciating pain engulfed him. Somehow he clambered back to the trail he'd come on but he had to drag himself. He could put no weight at all on that right leg. It shrieked with agony every time he tried to move it. How would he ever get back to the cabin, he thought as he lay there in the snow.

Though it really wasn't very far, it took Erick almost an hour of pain before he reached the cabin door. Trying to use a broken branch as a cane failed completely. Either it broke or the end of it sunk in the snow so far it couldn't support him. Eventually he fought the door open and slumped into his chair. If only he had a bottle of whiskey to kill some of the pain.

What to do? Trying to get to town for help was impossible. The chances of anyone visiting him were zero. There was enough soup to last for a few days more and he could put the rabbit in it with potatoes to make a stew. But could he keep warm? The woodbox was almost empty. Somehow he'd have to haul in some chunks and small wood and kindling. That meant he had to have a crutch of some sort. Maybe the old stub of a broom would do. Erick tried it out with the brush end in his armpit but the other end went too deeply into the snow to provide any support. Perhaps by crawling and then throwing the wood before him he could manage. Then Erick got the idea of nailing the cover of a coffee pail on the upper end of the broom. This meant sawing off the end of the handle. The pain was so fierce he could feel it behind his face but finally he got the crutch made so he could get in enough wood to last the night. Erick slept little that night. Spent most of it watching Nikki, now released from his box, dancing in the flickering light from the holes in the stove you use to lift the lids.

The next morning, when it finally came, was again full of pain. Once Erick had broken his arm trying to crank an old Model-T Ford and he remembered that Dr. Gage had set it and then put splints to hold the bones tightly together until it healed. Again in agony the old hermit hopped to the woodshed to bring back an armful of cedar kindling. Selecting some straight pieces and a strip of old blanket, he stood on that leg until he cried, then bound the leg first with the blanket tightly, then fastened the strips of kindling with fishline. Then he lay in his bunk only getting out of it when he had to do so. "Sisu!" he commanded himself. "All evils end!"

Many days passed before they did. They really ended when Annie Anderson, our postmistress, noticed that Erick hadn't picked up his pension check as he always did the first of the month. When John Pesola came for his mail one day, Annie told him about it. "I'm worried about old Erick," she said. "I know he sometimes has coffee with you when he comes to get his pension check the first of the month but it's been eight days after that now. Maybe you'd better go and check on him." In Tioga we took good care of our own, whoever they might be.

So one Saturday soon after that John Pesola snowshoed in to Erick's cabin in Horseshoe swamp, and then later snowshoed in again with Okkari and his sledge with ski runners to haul the old hermit back to town so Dr. Gage could treat him. Before they put Erick on the sledge he put all the barley and korpua he had left on the table for Nikki.

When my father examined Erick he told him he'd done a fine job of splinting, that he couldn't have done a better job himself. It was a simple fracture, he said, not a compound one, and the bones had already begun to knit. Dad put on a walking cast and told them to take Erick back to the swamp. He said it would hurt for a couple of weeks and to keep off it all he could.

So Erick came home again to his tight little cabin in the swamp and when he called "Tulla Nikki! Tulla Nikki" the little kangaroo mouse popped out of the knothole and did a wild dance of joy for him.

THE BIGGEST POTATO

Perhaps you remember Eino Tuomi and Emil Olsen, the Damon and Pythias of Tioga. They were the closest of friends, hunting, fishing and working together but each living in his own cabin separated from each other only by a garden. Eino had the cow and did the baking for both of them; Emil had the chickens and did the canning of berries, applesauce and venison. He kept the marinating barrel of dynamited fish in his shed, while Eino had the smoked fish hanging from his. They dug and planted and harvested the garden together.

Sometimes it was hard to believe they were such good friends because they argued constantly, Emil, the old Norwegian, bellowing and Eino, the old Finn, just quietly and tenaciously repeating what he had just said over and over again until Emil gave up and listened. Perhaps you remember how Eino tapped the telephone pole on April Fool's Day or how Emil got skunked up at Pete Half-Shoes house or how Aunt Lizzie hornswaggled both of them into going to church for the first time in their lives and how they fled down our hill street clad only in their long winter underwear and their clompers.

Anyway, one April afternoon the two old buggers were down in Eino's basement sprouting the potatoes for the fourth and hopefully the last time.

The two men stored all their vegetables there because it had stone walls and a dirt floor while Emil's had board walls and a board floor. It was dark down there despite the yellow light from a kerosene lamp and neither relished the miserable job because the spuds were already softening and most of them were small.

"Eino, dammit," Emil said, "Next year, no this year, let's grow bigger potatoes. These are not worth sprouting."

"Yah," said the old Finn, "but everytime you come over for potatoes you take the big ones and leave the little ones."

"You're crazy, Eino. I take little ones too."

"No, you don't but I've hidden enough bigger ones for seed."

Well that was something to argue about again. "Small ones can make big potatoes just as good as big ones can," said Emil. "In the old country, my mother used to save the peelings, and even they made big potatoes, and the small ones were just as good as the big ones. You just had to put four or five of them in a hill."

Eino said, "Big potatoes make big potatoes. Little potatoes make little potatoes. Big potatoes make big potatoes and little..."

Emil knew he didn't have a chance. "OK, OK!" he roared. "Maybe so, maybe so. All I want is we get more big potatoes this year. Tell you what I do. I bet you a bottle of Higley's whiskey I can grow a bigger potato than you can. I plant my row on one side of garden by my house and you plant yours on other side."

"And the one who grows the biggest potato gets the whiskey, yah," said Eino. The two men shook hands, knowing full well that the loser would share that whiskey as they had shared everything else for so many years. At least it was something to look forward to when the April snows still covered the land.

But those snows went swiftly and by the first of May they were gone. The first flowers, the marsh marigolds which we always called cow-slips, had lifted their yellow cups in the swamp pools. Then came the trailing arbutus, both white and pink, in which we could bury our noses and know it was truly spring. When its tiny flowers browned, the woods burst into bloom: wild iris (blue flags), Indian moccasin, lady slippers, pink, yellow and more rarely, pure white, adders tongues, blood root and Dutchman's Britches, jack-in-the-pulpit, blankets of spring beauties, trilliums, and of course the violets. The white violets came first, then the blue and violet, and finally the yellow ones. Nowhere on earth can there be a spring as lovely as that which comes to the U.P. Almost worth the winter!

By the third week in May the ground was dry enough to plant the gardens — and the potatoes. Oh the arguments that ensued! Eino generously brought out the big potatoes he'd hidden and offered to share them with Emil. "No!" said the big Norwegian. "Them Green Mountain potatoes we've been planting make too many small ones. I going plant Red Cobblers in my row."

"Red Cobblers don't keep so good and they full of bumps," objected Eino over and over again but Emil hiked up to Fred Longchamp's farm by the North Mine and came back with seven huge red ones. He offered one to Eino but the latter refused. "White potatoes best," he said, and that began another argument.

Then they argued about how to cut the seed pieces and how long they should dry and season in the sun before they were ready to plant. One good sprout on a piece, said Emil. No, at least two and better three, insisted Eino. Two days in the sun were enough to toughen the skin on the cut edge so they wouldn't rot? "No, three day, maybe four. In Finland always four," answered Eino.

As the cut potatoes dried, each man prepared his own row for planting. All Emil did was to dig a seven inch wide hole that was only about six inches deep, spacing the holes about two feet apart along the sixty feet of row where last year the peas had been planted. Eino thought that was too far apart, saying that only thirty hills apiece wouldn't yield enough to last the winter. One foot apart would be better, but in the end he gave up and used the same spacing.

However, Eino didn't make little individual holes for his potatoes, nor did he dig them in the old garden soil. Instead he began to dig a trench, one foot deep and one foot wide in new soil at his edge of the garden. "You crazy!" objected Emil. "Why so much work for nothing?"

"You'll see. You'll see," replied the little Finn, slicing off the sod and putting it on one side of the trench, then digging out the rest of the dirt to heap it up on the other side.

"You think you still mining, I guess," remarked Emil. "You nuts for dig so deep. Potatoes lie just under surface. Roots don't. Roots don't. And I put manure down deep, then put on sod, then more dirt from under cow manure pile, then surface dirt, then potato, then plain dirt."

"Oh, for dumb!" exclaimed Eino. "You think you plant roses, I guess. It's potatoes, not roses, you dumb Norwegian. Too much work!"

It was a lot of work and Eino was pooped when at noon he and Emil went into the Finn's house for a lunch of fresh baked bread, milk and a chunk of bologna. The butter was still pale, almost white. Cows needed green grass to make yellow cream and butter. Emil tore into the meal but Eino was too tired to eat. "Eino getting old," he said. "I go sleep a little before I finish."

By the time he awoke, finished his little meal and went to the garden, he found that Emil had dug all the rest of the trench and had enlarged his own potato holes. "You good friend, Emil," he said and the Norwegian answered, "Yah, you good friend too, Eino but you stupid dumb. Next time make holes like me."

The next argument had to do with what fertilizer to use. Now, back then in the early years of this century, there was no chemical fertilizer, just manure, but what kind was best for potatoes? Emil was for that from chickens. Eino insisted it was too strong, that it would burn and cook the potatoes right there in the ground or else it would produce big vines and few if any potatoes. He'd tried it once, he said. "Well, how about horse manure, then?" Emil asked. "We can get some from old man Marchand's pile..."

"No, no NO!" Emil was upset. "Horse manure burn too and full of weeds. Horse got only one stomach; cow have two to cook and kill weedseed. Garden pretty clean now; you put on horse crap and quack grass come right away all over."

"How come you know so much about horse shit?" Emil roared. "They got no horses in Finland — only reindeer. Maybe we go in woods and collect deer crap, eh?" So it went, on and on.

In the end, each man went his own way. Emil laid down a thin layer of chicken manure in his holes, covered it with two inches of garden dirt, covered that with an inch of humus from under the maple leaves, then made a shallow ring around each hole into which he put some more chicken manure. Also some pine needles for the seed potato chunk to sit on.

All afternoon the Finn labored hard with the wheelbarrow, bringing up cow manure from the oldest part of his pile to line the bottom of the trench. On this layer he then put the sod, grass side down, which he then covered with another layer of old cow manure. Next he covered that with about three inches of the new dirt he had dug from the trench. The trench was still six inches deep when he quit for the night but early next morning he covered the new dirt with a two inch layer of dirt, not manure, that he dug from under his manure pile. Black stuff, it was, and full of little red worms. Finally he shoveled in an inch of new dirt and called it a day. The trench was ready for planting at last.

The next morning they planted their seed potatoes, Emil his Red Cobblers and Eino his Green Mountains, but not until after another hot argument. The old Swede covered his with only two inches of soil but Eino used three or four. "Yours too shallow," Eino said. "They'll get burned by sun and turn green." Emil told him no, that all he had to do was put on more dirt and that Eino would be lucky if even two or three of his spuds ever saw the light of day.

Several weeks went by before Emil one early morning pounded on the Finn's door. "Wake up, Eino," he roared. "Come see!" A row of little green rosettes had appeared in Emil's row. "Yah, I tell you not to plant so deep. Norway forever!" Not a potato had come up in Eino's row, but Eino wasn't worried. "Mine come soon," he said, "and they have big roots and big roots make big potatoes, and whiskey for me." One week later his prediction came true. But then Eino did something that completely baffled Emil. He shoveled dirt over all those newly appeared potatoes.

"Why for you do that, you crazy Finn?" Emil asked. "Why you smother them when they need sun?"

"In old country we always cover new potatoes," Eino answered. "Makes them strong. You'll see!" Indeed they did break through the covering in a few days and looked very good. A few cold days ensued and there was a threat of frost one night. Emil took all his blankets off the bed, and all the old potato sacks, to cover his row. Had to build a hot fire and sleep in his clothes. Eino just covered his potatoes again with new dirt.

It tool almost a week before Emil's potatoes recovered from the flattening they got from the blankets he'd used and by that time Eino's had almost equalled them in height. Now it was time for hilling them up. When the old Finn saw how Emil was doing it, just hoeing heaps of dirt to mound them, he said, "No, Emil. You doing all wrong. You got loosen soil first before you heap." He took the hoe from Emil and demonstrated. "Big potatoes need soft dirt." After quite an argument Emil did the rest of his holes as Eino had told him. Eino banked his vines with dirt from under his manure pile.

Then came the potato bugs, the Colorado beetles. Now back then, in the early years of this century, there were few pests. No one ever sprayed an apple tree, for instance, because at harvest the apples were unblemished. Even today one can occasionally find a wild apple tree near an old lumber camp that still shows no signs of disease or codling moth damage. But we did have potato bugs galore. I remember being paid a penny for every ten of the yellow-bellied, black striped adults, another penny for every twenty leaves whose undersides were covered with yellow eggs or pink and orange baby bugs. I'd drop them in a can half full of kerosene, then after my father had looked them over and paid me, I'd set fire to the can and cremate them.

Most of our people coped by just picking the bugs like I've described but some emptied out the cuspidors or soaked a can of snuff to make juice which, when much diluted, they could sprinkle over the leaves of the potato plants. Others who had more money bought a box of Paris Green to mix with rain water. That worked better than the tobacco juice and it left a shiny residue of poisonous looking green on the upper sides of the leaves. The trouble with both methods was that the undersides of the leaves where the eggs and young were deposited were left untouched, so you had to spray and spray again. No, I don't mean spray; we had no sprayers then; we used sprinkling cans.

As you can imagine, there was plenty of argument between Emil and Eino about which method to use. Neither had money for the Paris Green nor did either own a sprinkling can. So the Norwegian soaked half a package of Peerless smoking tobacco in a big pail of water, made a little broom of chicken feathers, and brushed the leaves with the brown liquid. Took Emil half a day but Eino spent a whole day picking off all the bugs and egg-filled leaves from his row, and then had to do it all over again several times because new bugs from Emil's row kept invading once they'd hatched from the underside of the leaves. He became so angry that he refused to go trout fishing with his friend one afternoon but the anger melted when Emil came back with six ten-inch brook trout, fried them crisp, and invited him over for supper. Eino noted that Emil had cut the heads off before cooking the fish which puzzled him. Always they'd been left on.

He found out why the next day when three of Emil's potato hills had little holes in them. "Yah, the old Norwegian grinned. "I bury two fish heads in each hill for extra fertilizer but skunk come last night and dig them out. All's fair for whiskey!"

Finally Eino's vines were just as tall as Emil's but the latter's blossomed first making a long row covered with pink-purple flowers. When they faded and dropped off, Eino's blossoms came, all white ones. Making a jar of sugar-water, he patiently dipped a little of it on each blossom. Emil thought he was nuts and said so, but soon many bees were hovering over the patch. "Bees in flowers make big fruit," said Eino.

This coincided with one of the rare drouths that come to the U.P. For two weeks not a drop of rain fell. Knowing that blossom time and shortly thereafter is when the tubers are forming, both men hauled many pails of water from the well to soak the hills at this crucial time. One time Eino soaked his with manure tea after dumping some fresh cow manure in his rain barrel and stirring it up thoroughly. "That's crazy!" said Emil, observing. "How you going to get clean clothes now?" "I clean barrel," was the reply. Eino did one other thing too that made no sense to the old Norwegian. He got the rest of the swamp hay from the hay mow, now that the cow was in pasture, tucked it around the base of each of his potato plants, and then watered the hay too. "You dumb Finn," Emil roared. "Why you keep sun off? Potatoes need sun." But he had to keep watering more often than his friend did, and pulling more weeds.

One evening Emil saw Eino down on his knees, digging with his hands in a few hills , and pulling out some baby potatoes. Again he was sure the Finn had gone insane. "Let them grow! Let them get big!" he yelled.

"I get hungry for new potatoes," Eino answered. "Little ones the best." (And they are, too, especially when creamed.) But the real reason Eino was doing it was because he figured that if he pulled off the little ones and left the bigger ones, the latter would get more food and so grow bigger. "Yah," he chuckled to himself. "All's fair with love and potatoes."

July soon passed, and August month. No frost yet but Emil's vines had begun to shrivel and get brown. Not Eino's. They were thick and green and sturdy. "Give me two, three weeks and I get whiskey for sure," he said to himself.On September eleventh we got clobbered by a frost so heavy that even the grass was still white by noon. In the U.P. we call that the black frost because it blackens everything, everything except the forest which soon turns to a luminous symphony of scarlet and gold.

It was time to dig the potatoes. The first hill that Emil dug he got a potato so huge he pranced around hollering something like "Sittin de mai." It wasn't a pretty potato, being knobby, but it must have weighed a pound or more. Eino's first hill yielded about twelve large potatoes and two small ones but none of them came close to that first one of Emil's. The two men spaded very carefully, not wanting to slice any of them. A few potatoes always seem to lie beyond the hill in their own chambers and often they are big ones so the men always began spading far out before they lifted. I always loved to dig potatoes though I hated hoeing them. Earth's bounty. It was like digging for gold. To see how one little piece of potato could beget a lot of fat children always seemed miraculous. Sure was enjoyable.

Eino hit real gold on his third hole, one of those from which he'd stripped the small potatoes. It wasn't as big around as Emil's big Cobbler but it was almost a foot long and very wide. No scab. The eyes were flat and smooth. Almost the Perfect Potato. Eino stroked the dirt from its skin and showed it to Emil whose face fell when he saw it. But as he dug hill after hill, he turned up many other Red Cobblers almost as big as his first one. What a harvest! Those spuds lay there gleaming in the sun all along the row. Never had they had so many big potatoes for the winter. Almost worth the work even if they lost the whiskey. It was hard to say, until measuring, which man had the biggest. Each new hill gave promise that in it the biggest potato would appear. Yet they quit before they dug the last hill, as they'd agreed to do long before. That was their "hope hill", or "last hope hill." They'd dig that one tomorrow.

After lunch the two men sorted their potatoes, turning each one so the damp bottom side would also cure in the sun. One area held the really big ones, the monsters; another the ordinary big ones; and the third the few little ones. Then they had to choose which of the monsters was the biggest. Took a lot of time to decide. Once again a hot argument broke out, Emil holding that the biggest one in circumference was naturally the biggest. Not so, said Eino, the biggest is the longest. Or the heaviest? Worn out from arguing they selected the best potato monster they had and took it up to M.C. Flynn's store to be weighed on the meat scale. Emil's best weighed exactly one pound and fifteen and a half ounces. So did Eino's. Maybe one of their other monsters might weigh a bit more. They did some sorting but in the end, they agreed it was a tie. All depended on that last hill they'd dig tomorrow. Both felt that he might have a chance. Emil had peed on his every time he had to go out at night. Eino had given his hill extra manure and also cow milk in the water.

The next morning they dug their last hills. Emil sure worked carefully before he scooped out the monster of monsters, a twin potato so big that it was certain the whiskey was his. (I've grown a few twin potatoes though they are rare. They're two full grown potatoes joined by a common neck.) The twins on this monster, though, were as huge as the one Emil had brought up to be weighed at Flynn's store. Never had there been so big a potato!

"Yah," said Eino. "I think you win whiskey. I never see so big a potato, but I dig my own last hill first before I give up." He dug and he dug and finally unearthed a potato almost three feet long. Twenty smaller potatoes were strung along a peeled stick looking like a shish kabob. Then Eino took Emil's twin potato and showed that it also had been made by joining two big potatoes on a peeled stick.

They both began to laugh, helplessly. "OK, OK," Emil said. "How you know I make one of two?"

"Last night after I put out the light, I sit by window looking at moonlight," Eino replied. "I smoking pipe there long time when I see you digging in garden, then coming my house to cut branch from hazelnut bush by back door.

So I go over your house and peek in window and see you putting potatoes together, then later planting them again. So I just make myself a bigger one yet. You got one more jar venison? We make a stew, eh?" A few hours later they washed it down with joint whiskey.

THE FORTUNETELLER

I suppose that all villages have an amateur fortuneteller or two who read Tarot cards or tea leaves to tell what's going to happen to you in the future. But Tioga had a pro, a real, genuine fortuneteller, Madame Olga. She returned to our village, where she was born, at the age of 67 when she could no longer bear the rigors of the traveling circus and carnivals in which she had spent her life. Too much arthritis. She'd saved a few thousand dollars and hoped that they would be enough to last.

I got to know Madame Olga through my friend Fisheye who, for fifty cents a week, tended her garden and chickens, cut and hauled in her wood, watched over the old lady and listened to her wondrous tales. Every time I got the chance I'd help Fisheye with his chores so I could hear her stories. Madame Olga loved to talk and needed listeners so we really got an education about a fascinating world under the tents. Both of us were so impressed we decided we'd join the circus or carnival as soon as we could, and sometimes I'm sorry that I never did.

I'll try to piece together my memories of what she told us about her interesting life. Olga Beauvier, the only daughter of a French Canadian couple who had a good solid whitewashed log cabin down in Frenchtown in the valley, had always been an adventurer and rebel. After graduating from High School, she took the train for Milwaukee immediately and became a housekeeper for her uncle, a bachelor, who owned a hardware business there, so she could know what city life was like. Very beautiful and vivacious, she evidently had a ball on her off hours with a series of admirers whom she exploited to the utmost, but never loved. After two years with her uncle, Olga was taken by one of her admirers to the Ringling Brothers Circus and was immediately smitten by the bands, the acrobats, the rides, the sideshow freaks, the elephants and lions. On an impulse she applied for a job, any kind of a job, got one as a ticket taker, and began a new glamorous life that lasted forty years.

"Ah, my sons," she would reminisce. "The excitement! The color! The sounds! Never can I forget. The team work. The calliope! Everyone knew his job or jobs. Most of us had several. I had to learn to ride a horse bareback and stand up on it as we circled the ring with the band playing and me in spangled tights with a helmet covered with brilliants looking beautiful. And the applause! Sometimes I was a clown with heavy make-up hitting my partner with my broom to make little children laugh. One time I rode elephants for a month looking pretty way up there on the beasts. I sewed sequins on costumes. No two days alike. Then the long train rides to strange cities I'd never heard of. Pack and unpack, put on the show, take down the tents and do it again. Always excitement." I can still see Madame Olga in her rocking chair on the side porch talking to Fisheye and me on the steps. A white turban around her grey hair, a purple dress, and bright red slippers made quite a sight as she gestured animatedly. Once when she blew a kiss to the days that had passed she winced and cried out in pain, because of the arthritis I suppose, but she talked and talked while we listened entranced.

Fisheye asked her about the circus freaks. "Don't you call them freaks, mon petit," she commanded fiercely. "They had differences, yes, and made their living by them, but never have I known such gallant, fine people." Madame Olga told us a lot about them but I forgot most of it. At one time she thought she had fallen in love with the Human Skeleton, a tall man whose bones rattled in his skin. A very sweet man, she said, but not of the marrying kind. She told of the Wild Man from Borneo who scared the liver and lights out of the people who came to his tent to see his act. Really, a gentle man, she said, who, despite his ferocious appearance, was deathly afraid of mice, just like the elephants were. And the contortionist who practiced constantly and once got so tangled up, with his legs brought over his shoulders and crossed, that two roustabouts had all they could do to put him back in normal shape. Always the fraternity and comradeship. One big family.

Some of her tales were scary, too. Once a main spar holding up one side of the big tent broke during the lion act and that whole side of the tent came down. Screams and pandemonium. Another time they had a fire under the stands and the elephants panicked. Madame Olga had seen a black leopard go berserk and kill its trainer. Once the circus train had derailed in the night. At a time when there were no radios or television and only an occasional flickering movie Madame Olga's stories enthralled us. There was another magical world out there. Someday Fisheye and I would enter it.

One Saturday Madame Olga had a task for us. We were to set up her fortune-telling tent in the side yard by the raspberries. It needed airing lest the mildew spoil it and besides she was considering taking it to the Marquette County Fair the next month to make a few dollars which she badly needed. Perhaps she would hold a few fortunetelling seances right here in Tioga first to see if she could bear the arthritis and to polish up her old skills.

The tent was in her loft along with several worn trunks. It was very heavy but Fisheye and I finally managed to get it down the stairs and into the side yard. Madame Olga, using two canes, painfully came down the steps to supervise. The poles were jointed and we had trouble fitting and locking them together as well as putting them up under the canvas but under her guidance we succeeded. About eight by ten feet and seven feet high, it sure looked good there in the yard with its black and white stripes. Madam Olga made sure we staked it properly and tightened up the guy ropes.

"Now bring down the green trunk," she ordered. Phew, that was a hard job too, it was so heavy, but we finally got it in the tent and opened it to find two collapsible chairs, a collapsible little table and a lot of black velvet coverings. Oh yes, and also a carved wooden box which, when opened, contained a beautiful black glass ball about four inches across. When you moved it, something swirled inside. Following the Madam Olga's directions we draped the table with the black velvet, put a white doily on top of it, and set the black ball on that. Then we placed an incense burner on each side of the ball. Madame Olga said she was ready for business but too tired just then to tell our fortunes but if we'd come back that afternoon, she'd do it. When she gave Fisheye his fifty cents she apologized for not being able to pay me too. "My money it is running out fast," she said. I told her I didn't want any pay, that I just liked hearing her circus stories.

That afternoon, when Fisheye and I returned, we found Madame Olga all dressed up in gypsy costume sipping some tea. I asked her how she became a fortuneteller and for more than an hour she regaled us with the tale.

It had all come about, she said, because once on her day off she had her own fortune told by no less than The Great Ozymandius, at that time perhaps the most famous fortuneteller in the land. She had been fascinated by the man and his uncanny knowledge of her life. She had been born in a log cabin, he told her, by a big lake. She had run away from home to seek her fortune in the city but had only found employment as a domestic servant for a man with a bald head. She had no brothers or sisters. She would soon be marrying an older man with a very black beard and would travel with him from ocean to ocean. She would have no children.

It was all true, Madame Olga said, and in three weeks she had married The Great Ozymandius whose beard was black as tar.
He needed an assistant as well as a wife so he trained her and imparted to her all of his secrets. At first, she spent many weeks listening behind the other compartment of their tent as her husband told fortunes, or she served as a shill or barker to get the gullible to seek his services. The Great Ozymandius insisted that he had no special powers to foresee the future but that he'd learned how to read the body language of his clients and how to hypnotize some of them, and also himself. There were two parts to fortunetelling, he told her. First, you had to tell them things about themselves that only they could know. This was done by scrutinizing the clients to see how they agreed or disagreed with any statement made by the seer. Sometimes it would be as obvious as the shake or nod of the head but usually it was the way they held their mouth or breath or other little signs meant yea or nay. Once he had learned these signs, he then started his patter, making tentative statements that could be completed in different ways, depending on whether the client

showed signs of agreeing or not. If he agreed, then you continued guessing along the same line; if not, you took a new tack.

Fisheye and I didn't understand and Madame Olga knew it, so she gave a simple example. "Suppose I've already found out that the man is married but want to tell him how many children he has. I would watch him carefully as I said, 'As for children...' and if I see the sign for no, I would tell him that he didn't have any. But if I see the sign for yes, than I would say, 'You have one...two...three' and keep going till I get a yes response, and then I'd tell him how many he had. You follow up your leads, always watching for the yeas and nays. It's not easy to do but I learned from a master and became very good myself. One of the hard things for me was pretending to read their palms when I was really reading their face and body looking for positives or negatives."

Madame Olga told us some almost unbelievable things that she had discovered during the sessions, that one man had killed his wife, that a woman had tried to commit suicide three times and was planning another attempt. "Sometimes it almost scared me," she said. "They tell their own fortunes by their sign language. I just put it into words," she insisted.

"But how do you predict the future, Madam Olga," I asked.

"Oh that's the easy part," she answered. "Much easier than telling them who they are. For one thing, they can't know what's going to happen, and I'm far away before they find out. By the time I go to the crystal ball for my trance to read their future, I already know quite a lot about them so I just guess what will occur."

"What's a trance?" asked Fisheye.

"I don't know," said Madame Olga. "The Great Ozymandius called it self-hypnosis. Sometimes I have to fake it, but usually I can go into a fortune-telling trance by looking into the black ball, prolonging the end of my breath and saying 'Oom' over and over again to myself. Then, when I get the feeling I'm half conscious, I start my mouth going and say almost anything that comes into my head in a strange voice until I run out of things to say. Then I wake up or pretend to and ask them what I've told them. Often the things they remember are the things they want to happen or are scared might happen. It's not easy work; it drains you because you have to be so alert. Haven't done any of it for three years now and perhaps I've lost my skill. That's why I want to tell your fortunes. But now a little wine."

Fisheye was the first to have his fortune told while I waited outside the tent. He came out radiant. "She told me I was going to be a soldier," he said, "and fight way over the ocean in a strange land. And that I would be an officer in command of many men." (Fifty years later he retired from the army with the rank of colonel.)

When I entered and sat down across the table from Madame Olga the smell of incense was overpowering. She took my hand and in a strange voice told me all about myself as she traced the lines and bumps. Nothing new; nothing that anyone in Tioga wouldn't have known. But then, after a long silence when she stared into the black crystal ball, Madame Olga came out with a torrent of words about my future. Her black eyes seemed glazed as sentence after sentence flowed from her lips. Finally, she shook herself and came out of the trance. "Tell me what I said," she commanded.

Lord, I couldn't remember half what she had told me. I would fly on a silver bird to lands far beyond the ocean. (This was in the days when the Wright Brothers had just made their first flights and I doubt that Madame Olga even knew about them. But she spoke truly. I have flown to many foreign lands, from Australia to the tip of Scandinavia and between.) Also she had said, "I see a great audience in a great hall and you are speaking to them. And when you are finished they all stand up and applaud." (This too has happened.) In that black crystal ball she had also seen me in a white suit being married. (A self-fulfilling prophecy? I did wear a white suit. Was it because of her prediction?) I would have three children, two girls and a son, and many grandchildren, (True!) In the swirls of that ball she had seen me on a great white ship on a sea surrounded by great mountains. (I have been on a white ship going up the Inland Passage to Alaska.) But the most amazing thing, one which at the time seemed absolutely nonsense, was this. "I see you at the piano playing on the keys while many sheets of music keep unrolling from it. I see a room with many books. I see your name on a blue book." (Madame Olga couldn't have known about typewriters or that here in my book lined study are thirty-two that I have written.) I'm sure that there were other predictions that haven't come true. At least not yet. (One of them was that I would have three wives and a red dog.)

Madame Olga seemed very tired when the seance was over and we had to help her get back to the house. "I don't know," she said. "Maybe I'm too old." She seemed exhausted.

Although she had planned to put up a sign in the post office advertising her fortunetelling services, she did not do so. Instead she went to bed for a week, finally sending up word to have my father, Dr. Gage, come to see her. After a thorough examination, he told her that her heart was fine and she'd probably live a long time. "But I can't, Doctor," Madame Olga said. "My savings are about gone. I am ready to die. Living in pain is no life." Dad gave her some of his purple aspirins and told her she must eat more, that she was badly malnourished, and would have to regain her strength before trying to earn a little money telling fortunes. Then he went to her neighbors asking them to visit her and help her. In Tioga we took care of each other.

Life was better for Madame Olga after that. The priest, Father Hassel, visited her, and mobilized his parishioners to bring her soup and food and gay conversation. Fisheye refused his weekly fifty cents but did all her chores and more. He and I often dropped in to get her talking about the old days but it was obvious that she was depressed and failing. Only Fisheye's Tante (Aunt) Cherie, an old childhood friend, seemed to be able to cheer her up, and discovering this, she came every day for conversation and to do the dishes and make the bed.

Later that month Fisheye's aunt had brought a bottle of chokecherry wine, a hunk of cheese, and a loaf of crusty French bread and the two old ladies were feeling the wine when Tante Cherie proposed that Madame Olga read her own fortune in the crystal ball. Madame Olga objected at first. "How can I do that?" she asked. Cherie suggested that she put the long mirror on the chair so she could see herself across the table. "But how will I know what I have said when in my trance?" she objected. "I will sit in the corner and tell you," her friend replied.

So, after the bottle was emptied and she had put on her gypsy clothing, the ball was brought out. It was very difficult for Madame Olga to get into the trance. Too many giggles at first. But at last her eyes began to glaze and her breathing slowed down. She swirled the ball and began to speak in that strange voice. Suddenly she shook herself and giggled again. "What did I say, Cherie? What did I say?" she asked.

"You say that you will soon be travelling again. On a train. And that you will be very rich."

"Ah, Cherie. It is as the Great Ozymadius, my husband, used to say. It's all humbug, hocus pocus. You tell the suckers what they want to hear. Oui, I want to travel again. I want to stop worrying about money. That is all impossible, of course, except in dreams."

But the very next day Annie, the postmistress, brought down a registered letter to Madame Olga. It was from Johnson, Beeman and Jones, Attorneys at Law, Milwaukee, Wisconsin, telling her that she had just inherited her uncle's estate of $342,000 but would have to come there to sign the necessary papers.

The Great Ozymandius was wrong. Madame Olga took the next train for Milwaukee and never returned to Tioga. Fisheye's aunt had a card from her from Arizona and that was all. It said, "Having a fine time spending money. Arthritis isn't bad. Dreams come true."

MY FRIEND RUDY

Shortly after supper on December the first, 1905, two babies were born in Tioga. I was one of them and Rudoph Salmi was the other. Fortunately our homes were right across the street so my father was able to deliver both of us without difficulty though it kept him humping, he said, because both of us arrived within the same hour.

Back then all babies were born at home but Rudy was born in a hospital, my father's hospital. This occurred because the Salmis lived in its west wing, his father being the hospital's male nurse and his mother, the housekeeper, who kept it spotless. They were first generation Finns who had come to this country in the late 1890's. Unable to speak a word of English, Saul and Vilma Salmi were met in New York by a cousin who helped them buy a ticket for Tioga, gave them a bag of food and taught them the English phrase "Where toilet?" He also pinned a card on each of them that said "Tioga Michigan." Another cousin met them at our village station, took them in and found Saul Salmi a job. They were only nineteen.

In 1900 when my parents came to Tioga it was not the little sleepy village it is today but a thriving town jumping with energy. Over a thousand men worked in its three mines and half again as many in the woods cutting the great white pine that covered the land. Tioga had been built from scratch in the forest and at that time was considered to be a model mining town. The Oliver Iron Mining Company which owned all the land had built a town hall, a clubhouse, a hotel (the Beacon House), a large boarding house, a three story school, many company houses all painted red and all identical, and a company-owned store to keep the people in debt. It built big frame houses for the mining superintendent, the mining captains, the school superintendent and the doctor, all of which were painted yellow. A few whitewashed log cabins built on rent-free land filled up the rest of our long hill street and there were many more of them on the side roads. Four churches took care of the souls of the inhabitants and three whorehouses and Higley's saloon handled their other needs. The mining company wasnt being albruistic in providing all these amenities; it just wanted to keep the men reasonably happy so they'd work twelve-hour day and night shifts for a dollar.

When my parents arrived in Tioga the Beacon House was full so they were given a suite above the operating room in the hospital consisting of a bedroom and a living room. They took all their meals at the hotel, a block away but living in that suite wasn't too pleasant for my mother to put it mildly. The only child of fairly wealthy parents, she had been reared in a city in lower Michigan and had attended finishing school to acquire all the social graces. To suddenly be plunged into a totally different and rough culture where more than half the people couldn't even speak English was very traumatic. Nevertheless she made the best of it.

My father, fresh out of medical school, loved the primitive land and its people. Dr. Beech, the company doctor, who had been overworked for a long time appreciated his services, taught him a lot about medicine, and gave him much responsibility. After my father had shot his first deer and caught his first trout he was hooked forever.

As she told the story to me many years later, those first months in Tioga were very difficult for my mother. She was very lonely and my father was absent most of the day and sometimes at night on a baby case. The groans and moans of the patients in the ward next to their suite were hard to bear and the screams of those in the operating room below her were worse. Desperate for female companionship she decided to hold a tea party for some of the young wives of the mining engineers and school teachers that she had met during their meals at the Beacon House. Fortunately she brought with her a complete tea service of Haviland china and she knew how to make tea though she'd never baked anything in her life. Since one had to have teacakes, she went up to the company store and bought tea and sugar, cream and two bags of different cookies, one of ginger snaps and the other of chocolate-covered cookies covered by gooey coconut. Unfortunately the cookies were so stale they were inedible.

Her mother had also given her a book of recipes and in it she found a cookie recipe that read as follows:
1 c butter; 1½c sugar; 3 eggs; 1 tsp baking soda diss. in 1½ T hot water; 3¼c flour; ½ c chopped raisins; ½ c chopped nuts; ½ c currants. Drop on buttered tin and bake at 350 degrees for 15 minutes.

39

Purchasing the ingredients, she went downstairs to the hospital kitchen where Vilma was doing the dishes from the noon meal for the patients.

"Paiva, Vilma," she said. (My father had taught her two Finnish words, *paiva* for hello, and *kituksia* for thank you.) "I'm going to have a tea party for some of my friends this afternoon and I wonder if you would show me how to bake some cookies." Vilma gestured helplessly and mother realized she hadn't understood a word. She tried again speaking very slowly and got the same response. When mother pantomimed stirring something in a bowl and pointed to the oven of the big hospital range, Vilma looked puzzled and said something in Finnish that left my mother helpless too. They looked at each other and laughed.

Then mother had an inspiration. "Come with me, Vilma," she said beckoning the Finn woman to follow her upstairs to the suite where she had already set the table with linens and fine china for the five women she'd invited. Vilma nodded her head with understanding. Then mother pretended to put some oolong tea in the silver teapot and to pour it into the cups. Again Vilma nodded. Opening the two bags of stale cookies she had purchased at the store, mother pretended to taste one, made a face of disgust, and put the bags in the wastebasket before pointing to ingredients for the cookies she wanted to make. Again she acted out putting them in a bowl and stirring. Vilma's face lit up. "Yo, yo (yes), she exclaimed pointing to herself and stirring in the invisible bowl. She understood.

After the two had brought the cookie stuff downstairs to the kitchen mother again pantomimed stirring and putting the batter in the oven. Vilma nodded but when mother picked up a towel to help dry the huge mound of dishes on the sink Vilma took it away from her. "Ei ei (No), she said, "Doktori vaino (wife) ei,ei." She made it clear that the doctor's wife wasn't to do any dishes by almost pushing her to the base of the stairs. Mother opened her little gold watch and pointed to the number four. Vilma nodded.

The tea party was a great success with good talk and merriment even though there were no cookies. Instead Vilma had baked a *pullaa*, a Finnish coffee cake. Never had they had such a marvellous coffee cake, mother's guests said, "so full of nuts, currants and raisins." Afterward, when mother went downstairs, she used the only other Finnish word she knew. "Kituksia, Vilma. Kituksia, Kituksia. Thank you so much," and kissed Vilma on the cheek, getting a big hug in return. They were friends.

That evening she told my father, "John, I've needed a project to keep me from being lonely and I think I have one. I'm going to learn how to speak Finnish and at the same time I'm going to teach Vilma how to speak English. I like her very much. Do you think it's possible?"

Dad was very supportive. "Of course," he replied. "You learned French and German in finishing school. Finnish won't be any harder. Just wish I could speak it. The only things I can say are "Where does it hurt?" and "How are your bowels?"

So thereafter each morning at ten o'clock Mother would go downstairs to have coffee with Vilma and the latter would come up to the suite every afternoon for tea about three. They began by building what a linguist would call a corpus, a basic vocabulary of terms for the things around them. Mother would write out the words she wanted to learn on a sheet of paper and Vilma would write down their Finnish equivalents. Chair was *tuoli*; oven was *yvni*;

hot was *kuuna*; match was *tullitikku* (Mother often had to borrow one to light the little alcohol stove on which she made her tea); fork was *hanko* and knife was *puuko* or *veitsi* and so on. They would practice saying them until they got the pronunciation right. Mother had trouble with the Finnish *y* as in *hyvasti* (Goodbye) and Vilma had trouble with the English *th* sounds. Fortunately, Finnish is a very phonetic language, each written letter always representing the same sound, and she mastered them more quickly than did Vilma because in English the written spelling is often very unphonetic. Since they only learned about ten words a day both made headway.

Then came the problem of putting words together in phrases and sentences. Mother solved that by writing out the sentences she wished to speak and then going across the road to Dr. Beech's house where they had a hired girl who spoke both English and Finnish. She wrote them down and coached her on how they should be spoken. That helped a lot.

By the end of three months the two women were able to understand each other part of the time; at the end of the year they had only a little difficulty. Mother had sent away for three books, a history of Finland, an English-Finnish, Finnish-English Dictionary and a copy of the Kalevala, the great Finnish epic which they began to translate into English. The two women by this time were very close friends.

Then Dr. Beech left for softer climes and the Oliver Mining Company gave his big house to my father, rent-free, together with all of its furnishings, two horses, a buckboard, a surrey with an actual fringe on top, and a cutter for winter driving. The move meant that mother had to learn to cook and do a lot of other things. Vilma's help was invaluable.

When, two years later, Vilma and my mother discovered about the same time that they were pregnant, they were delighted, at least until the morning sickness hit them. Nothing in my father's dispensary seemed to help so one day Vilma made a brew of some wintergreen berries "like they did in the old country," she said. Mother asked Dad if she should try it.

"Why not?" he replied. "Who knows? Some of these old folk remedies really work. I used one the other day on a woman with a stubborn urinary problem, two drops of turpentine on a spoonful of sugar. Heard about it from an old French Canadian woman. Anyway, it cleared up the problem." So mother drank the wintergreen brew and had no more morning sickness.

From the first, the lives of Rudy and me were closely intertwined. Each of us had two mothers. As soon as the winter abated, Mother would bring me over to the Salmis when she came for coffee and to speak Finnish. In the afternoon when Vilma came to our house to speak only English, she brought Rudy with her. Somewhere there are some old snapshots of Rudy and me in my playpen with our arms around each other but with blank expressions on our faces, and of the two babies in the Salmi's big crib sleeping peacefully together. The two friends loved to hold each other's baby and once when I was very restless Vilma put me to her breast to suckle. This shocked Mother but she did the same to Rudy. When my mother found that Vilma was dusting flour on Rudy's bottom she gave her a big can of talcum powder. In return, when Vilma found mother's diaper pail overflowing she took it home and returned it not only clean but with the diapers ironed. There also are pictures of the two of us crawling on the Salmi's rag rugs and on the Gage's carpets.

At first Rudy and I could play together only during our mothers' visits but as soon as we learned to walk and could be trusted to cross the street we were in each other's houses and yards all day, in his every morning and in mine every afternoon.

I don't really remember how we learned to talk but soon both of us were speaking each other's languages, always speaking Finnish in his home and English in mine. I dimly recall a game we played called *mita* which means "what?" We'd take turns pointing to something and if I correctly identified the big kerosene lamp with the red roses on its globe as *lamppu* after Rudy said *mita*, or a chair as *tuoli*, Rudy would hug me and then we'd roll around on the floor. If I got it wrong, he'd say "ei, ei" and correct me. Counting in Finnish was hard for me but I finally learned to say "yksi, kaksi kolme, nelja, and so on." I never learned to read or write Finnish so I hope the Finns who read this book will forgive my mistakes.

My *äiti* (Yes, I thought of her as my mother) always called me *Kalle*, the Finnish equivalent of Carl or Charles. Charles is my real first name but I was known all my childhood and youth as "Cully" and even my wife called me that for fifty years, hence the pen name I've used as the author of these Northwoods Readers.

I wish I could find words to describe our relationship. Rudy and I were not just the best of friends. We were much closer than brothers, perhaps as close as identical twins. We could play in my sandpile all afternoon making mines and never have an argument. Though often we wrestled and chased each other like bear cubs, we never once fought. We shared everything. If we went to pick wild strawberries or flowers for our mothers, we made sure that neither of us had a bigger handful. If we played marbles the winner always gave the marbles back to the loser at the end of the game. If one of us were hurt, the other cried too. I remember once that äiti caught us chasing chickens, a no no, gave Rudy a hard swat on the behind, and called him a "paha poika! (bad boy), which made him howl. I howled too and took her hand and made it hit me. She marched us back to her home, put us on the warm wide lap I loved so well, gave us a sugar lump to suck and sang us a Finnish lullaby till our tears were gone.

Rudy and I always helped each other do our little chores. We collected the eggs and fed the chickens and hauled in kindling and small wood to our mothers' kitchens. We put the potato bugs in a can that held some kerosene, then asked for a *tulitikku* (match) to set them afire and hear them sizzle.

But mostly we just played. In the winter we made snow forts but never threw a snowball at each other. In the spring we made snow dams in the wagon ruts and whooped when Mr. Marchand, our mail carrier's sledge broke them to let the water loose, or we sailed little shingle boats on the snow melt ponds in our yards. When summer came, we'd climb little saplings in the grove behind the hospital until they bent and let us down. We built crude little shacks in that grove and often would sit close together there in sheer happiness.

When occasionally we got permission Rudy and I would walk up to the mine, always hand in hand, to see the great wheels on the shaft houses bringing up the ore and the little tram cars hauling it out to dump on the huge ore piles. In the evenings when the bats circled overhead we'd try to catch one by flinging up our caps. Never caught one but we tried. Or we'd play aunty-eye-over, throwing a rag ball over the shed then running around to see who could find it first because whoever did could be the thrower. Sometimes we'd give each other the ball when we found it. Often at lunchtime we'd eat in each other's homes. Äiti cooked a dish consisting of creamed smoked fish on mashed potatoes which I dearly loved and there was a soft cheese called *juusto* that was delicious. But best of all were her hot cinnamon rolls, huge brown things with thin spirals of dough which we unwound slowly to get to the delectable heart. When Rudy ate at our house mother always played the piano afterwards and he and I, holding hands, would prance and dance wildly to the music.

When I was half past three my parents decided to enroll me in kindergarten because I was already reading childrens' books and perhaps they felt I needed playmates other than Rudy. It was a disaster. I hated every moment of school. Every morning I fought my mother when she insisted I go. There was a lot of anxiety too, wondering if Rudy would be there when I returned. Finally, after a month of it, the kindergarten teacher told my folks that I was still too young to profit from school so Rudy and I were together again.

A year later when both of us went to school, everything was fine. Rudy had a harder time than I because he was then learning how to read and write in both languages so I often helped him with his homework. I remember that when he misspelled a word and had to sit down, I misspelled my word on purpose so I could sit down too. At recess we played with each other, not with the other kids, and we protected each other. Once, when Pipu Viirta, a big kid, teased and hit me, Rudy swarmed all over him and together we got him down rubbing his nose in the dust until he fled away crying. Triumphant, we hugged each other all the way home.

Our seventh year was a delight. My father commissioned an old Finn to make a set of skis for both of us so the winter went swiftly. That summer we both learned to swim, or rather dog-paddle in the shallow water of Fish Lake. We hunted birds and chipmunks with slingshots but never killed any. We hiked down to the beaver pond and caught trout. We explored the edges of the forest. Comrades!

That fall a very virulent type of scarlet fever hit Tioga and Rudy and I contracted it on the same day. We were both very sick. I still remember the hallucinations I had, the cold cloths they kept putting on my forehead, the burning of the fever, the cool hands of my äiti and my mother. This happened long before there were any sulpha drugs or antibiotics and despite my father's heroic efforts several of his patients died.

Rudy was one of them.

When, after two weeks of very serious illness, I recovered enough to walk about, my mother told me. "Rudy was very sick too," she said weeping, "but he died and is in heaven." I could not believe it. "No!" I said. "No! No! He's right across the street." She tried to hold me but I broke away. When äiti saw me she too began to cry. *"Missa* (where) Rudy?" I asked her. "Can he come out to play?"

Äiti picked me up, hugged me hard, and rocked me in her arms as she weepingly told me that yes Rudy was dead, that he was in heaven, and that I'd never see him again. I wept unconsolably for a long time. It was impossible. Missa Rudy? Missa Rudy? Because every night I prayed hard to God that Rudy would be at his home when I went there, I said the same thing to Äiti morning after morning: "Missa Rudy? Can he come out to play?" but he wasn't there. Finally one day she took me to his little grave in the hill cemetery, showed me the small rock slab that said "Rudolph Salmi 1905-

1912)". We wept together and I wept again seventy years later when I saw that marker so hard to read.

I remember praying to God that he would take me up to heaven too so I could be with my friend. "Now I lay me down to sleep/ I pray the Lord my soul will keep/ If I should die before I wake..." Yes, dear Lord, let me die before I wake so I can be with Rudy in your heaven. But He didn't take me and for weeks I felt guilty just for being alive, for just being able to walk or to move a finger.

Few adults can comprehend the intensity of a child's grief when he has lost a loved one but I do. My world was empty. Half of me was gone. I had uncontrollable crying spells even in school. At home I would sit for hours pretending to be reading a book. Often I had fits of uncontrollable rage. It wasn't fair! It wasn't fair!

Then I had a period in which I couldn't bear to go across the road to see my äiti because it hurt too much. Instead I developed a fantasy life. Rudolph and I were the sons of Captain January, a lighthouse keeper. Day after day we would climb the circular stairs to fill the lamps with kerosene or to polish the big lenses. We'd sit for hours on the sand watching the big waves roll in. We'd put our arms around each other and talk. Sometimes when I was living this fantasy at home my parents worried because they couldn't get through to me.

Just as I was partially healing there came another blow. Suddenly one afternoon a great cave-in at the mine occurred, breaking the sidewalks and smothering the sun with a huge cloud of dust. The next morning officials of the mining company came down from Duluth, looked the situation over and decided to close the mine, close it forever. All the employees were dismissed, the hospital was closed, and the Salmis moved to Ishpeming.

I had lost my äiti too.

TO BED, TO BED, YOU SLEEPY HEAD

When Alf Jensen and Helga Svenson got married the whole town of Tioga was delighted. Never such a fine young couple. Made for each other, they were. Both were Scandehoovians. Alf was Norwegian and Helga was Swedish which might possibly cause some trouble but they had been sweethearts since grade school and never had any fights. No, it was a good match. Alf had inherited a fine house from his parents with a hayfield and barn and chickenyard. Helga had worked as a hired girl and cook for a rich family in Marquette for a year so she knew how to keep house. Alf had a good steady job as a section hand on the railroad. Yes, they'd have a good marriage and lots of kids.

The wedding in the Swedish Lutheran Church cost five dollars for rent, fifteen for the preacher who had to come up on the train from Ishpeming, two dollars for a license, and five more for the chivaree they knew would be forthcoming. Because all of us liked them it came mercifully early in the evening before they'd gone to bed and only lasted an hour or so. Helga made Alf a good snack before they retired and the loving was very good too. It had been a long day so Alf promptly fell asleep. Helga did not.

As Helga looked lovingly at that strong young man beside her in bed, she felt both happy and lucky. But not for long. Suddenly from his open mouth came a sort of catch, then a sudden throbbing inhalation. It was very loud and those that followed were louder yet. Then came a snort and a whistling noise and finally a bit of merciful silence. Helga closed her eyes seeking sleep but almost jumped out of bed when a whole series of snorts, gurgles, and nose grunts built up into a crescendo that rattled the rafters. Helga, with great effort, finally shook him awake.

"What's a matter? Alf asked sleepily.

"You snore so loud I can't sleep," replied Helga. "Turn over on your side." Alf did but he turned facing her and soon was snoring in her ear. She tried to turn him over the other way but he was too heavy to move, and he was snoring even worse, if that were possible. Finally she gave up and went into the kitchen to sit in the rocking chair by the stove.

Her thoughts were not pleasant ones. She had married a monster. She would never be able to get a night's sleep again. Did Alf know how awfully he snored? He should have told her. Could she ever get used to it? Maybe in fifty years. Without sleep she'd turn into an old hag. Self-pity and anger flooded over her. Was there any way to stop such terrible snoring?

Finally she went back to bed, pulling the covers over her head but that didn't help much. Then she tried to go to sleep with her fingers in her ears to block out the wheezes, croaking, sizzles and loud fluttering snorts but to no avail. She wanted to hit him in the mouth, to cork that open mouth with a dishrag. It infuriated her to see him sleeping so deeply and happily while filling the bedroom with bedlam. Her wedding night! And thousands more to go!

Helga probably did sleep a few winks or two but in the morning when Alf became amorous she refused his advances, telling him in no uncertain terms that she hadn't slept a bit all night because of his snoring. She did get up to stagger around the kitchen getting his breakfast but she told Alf he'd have to pack his own dinner pail, that she was so exhausted she was going back to bed. This she did and slept until noon.

That afternoon, revived, Helga baked bread and rolls and made a fine potroast supper to welcome Alf when he returned from work. Everything seemed perfect and the loving that night did too. After it was over Alf suggested that she go to sleep first, that he'd sit in the kitchen for an hour before coming back to bed. Ah, he was a good man, Helga thought, a kind one. They'd have a fine marriage after all. But she couldn't go to sleep, try as hard as she could, and was still wide awake when he came, lay down and started snoring immediately. It was another long, utterly miserable night for the new bride. Something had to be done.

The next day, Sunday, Alf didn't have to work so eventually they had the time for some straight talk. Helga asked him if he knew he snored so loudly before he proposed.

After long thought Alf answered. "Yah, I guess I knew but I never think of it. All I could think of was you, Helga. I don't ever hear myself snore so I don't know how it sounds. Last year, though, Iggy and Reino and Sven asked me to spend a week with them hunting deer by their cabin on the South Fork and after the first night in camp they kicked me out. Said I snored so loud none of them could sleep. So I guess I knew but didn't think to tell you. Would you have married me if you had known?"

Helga got up and put her arms around his neck from behind his chair. "Oh yah, Alfie. I marry you no matter what. I'll get used to it." But she asked him to make her some ear plugs. He spent most of the afternoon whittling them out of basswood. Little tiny things they were, fitted carefully to her ears with many kisses and wrapped in cloth saturated with beeswax. When she tried them out, Olga could barely hear what he said to her. They worked!

After more wonderful loving that night she put in the ear plugs and waited for that first horrible snore. It came soon enough but it was muted. She could hear it but it wasn't really very loud so Helga yawned and closed her eyes. Unfortunately she found that every time she yawned, or sometimes even if she swallowed, her ears ached and, being so tired, she yawned a lot. It's hard to keep from yawning or swallowing so, despite a few brief catnaps, Helga got up, took out the ear plugs, and tried to sleep in the rocking chair again. Another very long, miserable night, but by morning Alf found it hard to waken her when it was time to make coffee, probably because the ear plugs were in place. When Helga told him that again she had slept very little, he found it hard to believe her.

That evening before they went to bed Alf asked her to tell him or show him how he snored so he could understand what she had to put up with. Somehow she couldn't so she spent much of that night studying his snorings and making a list and practicing. Some were very hard to describe in words and a few she just couldn't imitate but the list she showed him the next morning and demonstrated went like this "catch, throat flutter, snort, whistle, gurgle and gargle, nose grunts, three kinds of moans, sizzle, sudden hoots or yelps." Alf was shocked. "No wonder you can't sleep," he said. "I didn't know it was so bad. You think you can ever get used to it?"

"I must," Helga replied. "But it's harder because you snore so many different ways. If you did it only one way it would be easy to blot out. But, Alf, I noticed too that you never snore if your mouth is shut - only when it hangs open. Maybe you got a crooked bone in your nose so you can't push much air out of it?"

"I'll try tonight to keep my mouth shut and breathe through my nose" said Alf, "and if that doesn't work I'll go see Dr. Gage and have him take a look. OK?" Helga nodded.

Helga almost felt sorry for her husband when that night he kept saying to himself over and over again, first aloud, then in a whisper and finally with only his lips moving, "Breathe nose; no breathe mouth." He really tried, Alf did, but tired from the days heavy labor he was soon asleep with the jaw hanging down and snoring hard and loud. Helga tried to get used to it, to ignore it, to think of other things or to try to bear the ear plugs longer but she was back in the chair again at midnight. Alf roused, found her gone, and sleepily staggered into the kitchen. "Oh Helga, I'm so sorry. I tried to keep my mouth shut but when I sleep I forget, I guess. Tie a scarf over my head and jaw so I won't open it." She was very touched by his concern and hugged him hard as she put on the scarf. He was a sweet man. But it didn't work. Kept slipping off.

True to his word, Alf went to see my father, the doctor, the next day and explained the situation. Dad was sympathetic and said snoring could be a real problem - especially in a new marriage. Then he cooled a little mirror with a long handle under a faucet and placed it under each nostril as he compressed the side of Alf's nose, first on one side, then the other. "No," he said, "There's no blockage." Putting on his headband with the big round mirror with a hole in it, Dad focussed some light on each opening to see if they were clear, and then had Alf open his mouth wide so the throat could be examined. "Your uvula, (that's the little thing that hangs down between your tonsils) is a bit long but not enough to cause the trouble. No, Alf" he said, "there's nothing organically wrong with you; there's no drug that can help either. Modern medicine has a lot of problems with no solutions and snoring is one of them. You don't have to feel guilt about it. Some men snore and some don't. There's no cure. Oh, I've heard that the old Finns have a cure but I don't know what it is. Probably just nonsense." Dad didn't charge Alf anything for the examination.

The next day Helga went to see our town's Wise Woman, Mrs. Matson, to ask if she knew the Finnish cure for snoring. "Yah," said the wise woman. "You get some limburger cheese or better yet the Norwegian gammelost which they ripen in a manure pile over the winter. Limburger stinks like hell and gammelost even worse. What you do is wait till he's in deep sleep and snoring, then you smear some of it just below the nose. Don't let him see you doing it or he'll hit you." The wise woman lit her corncob pipe. "Yah, works fine every time."

When Helga, desperate enough to try anything, went to Flynn's store, Mr. Flynn said he didn't carry any limburger or gammelost cheese. Never had and never would. They stank too much. But he told her that he'd heard the Leif Backe family still made gammelost in old country way and perhaps she could beg some from them. "Be sure to have them wrap it good," Mr. Flynn said, "or you'll stink up the whole town. Why you want that awful stuff?"

Helga didn't tell him but she did get a little jar of gammelost from the Backes. "Best to eat only a little of it on a lot of crackers and wash it down with aquavit fast," they advised her.

Helga didn't feel good about the whole thing but, desperate after having no sleep until three in the morning, she dipped her finger in the jar and gingerly smeared some of the soft cheese above his upper lip when he was snoring something awful. She was scared. Maybe Alf would hit her and, if he did, she wouldn't blame him. In just a moment, Alf's snoring stopped dead in its tracks. He snorted three times, then, without opening his eyes, he said, "Helga! Move down! Move down!"

"Move down!" The implication hit her like a rock. Helga wanted to kill him right there in bed but all she did was slap him hard across the face, sweep the deena (the goose down comforter) off her sleeping and again snoring husband, and weeping went to the kitchen to roll up in it by the stove. Her finger stank. She resolved that she would move out in the morning though she knew her family would not let her come home. No, not for a little thing like snoring. They would tell her she had made her bed and would have to lie in it. Divorce? No, that was impossible. No one got divorced in Tioga. She had no money.

Helga was still sobbing in the deena when Alf appeared. "Helga," he said, "You no stink. I stink. I make fire in sauna."

She got up and put her arms around him to confess what she had done and through her tears to beg forgiveness. No, he didn't hit her; he just picked her up in his big arms, took her to the bedroom and laid her gently down on the bed. Then he returned to the kitchen to sleep under the deena by the stove despite her protests. Too exhausted to argue, Helga fell immediately into a deep sleep from which she awakened at daylight to the smell of coffee and the stroking of a finger under her nose. When she opened her eyes there was Alf with a big grin on his face. "You snore so loud I can't sleep," he said.

He took the day off work, went to Ishpeming on the train, and brought back in the baggage car a single bed with mattress and springs. When Marchand our mailman, couldn't fit them on his cutter, Alf borrowed some rope and lugged them up the hill on his back. It took him three trips. Tioga wasn't at all surprised. All of us knew why he'd been kicked out of deer camp and it just made sense to have two beds when he snored like that.

So Alf and Helga slept happily ever after.

GRAMPA GAGE

Every nine or ten year old should have a grandfather like mine. Grampa Gage, who lived with us two summers when I was at that impressionable age, probably shaped me more than any other individual and not always for the better, may I say. At seventy-four, Grandpa was a short, wiry man with white hair and mustache who'd been a teamster in a logging camp, a grocer, and a bank president. Around our home and in public, he was very self-possessed and dignified but once he and I were alone that picture changed dramatically. A wild, zany companion he suddenly became, sometimes an Indian on the warpath, a hunter of lions in Africa, a bird, even a he-flea hunting for a she-flea and that's hard because as he said, "the flea is wee and mercy me, you cannot tell a he from she, but she knows well and so does he." Never have I known anyone with such a free-wheeling imagination. It was contagious.

Each morning Grampa and I shaved, then did our exercises before anyone else was up. He'd lather up both our faces, then shave himself with the gleaming edge of his long razor, then mine with the back of it. Always he kept saying, "I'm the mildest mannered man that ever cut a throat" so ferociously he almost scared me. His calisthenics were equally wild and varied. He'd put his old head between his legs to make faces and insist I do the same. He'd alternate swinging his arms over his head then wiggle his fingers with his thumbs in the opposite ear, or do his Dance of the Wild Cucumber. "Limber up the old bones, Mr. Bones!" he'd chant. Really quite a workout. Then he'd build a fire in the kitchen stove, put a pot of coffee on to boil, and we'd sit for a spell on the back steps enjoying the early morning sunshine.

That was when he gave me my name for the day. No, he never once called me Cully. I was either "Boy" or "Mr. Finnegan" or "Mr. O'Rourke" or had some other name. Once, after I'd been in a fist fight the evening before and had gotten a black eye, he dubbed me "Joshua" and all that wonderful morning Grampa and I fought the "Battle of Jerico When the Walls Came Tumbling Down." We climbed up on Mount Baldy, got stick swords and spears, and fought the Philistines all over that cliff, ending the battle by rolling big rocks over the edge and listening to them crash in the woods below. "Take that, Belshazzar," Grampa would roar. "Watch out, Joshua!" he'd yell. "There's four Philistines right behind you. Smite them, Joshua!" and then he'd come to my aid, walloping the trees and bushes and yelling war cries. Finally, when we were tired out, we counted the enemy dead and Grampa looked me over. "Only one walking wounded. That's not bad. Only one black eye!"

Grandpa Gage had found the secret of childhood: Let's Pretend! Most of us, as we grow up to get clobbered by reality, forget that secret and our lives are the worse off because of that forgetting. Only a few of us are lucky enough to have retained it. "All those who believe in fairies, clap their hands!" I clap mine and I hope you do yours. Certainly Grampa did. One morning he said to me, "Mister Hogan, I've a mind to find a big raven today, climb on its back, and take an aerial voyage. Will you join me, sir?" Again we went up on Mount Baldy and searched around until he found a long black boulder. "Ah," said he. "Here's our raven. Shall we board, Mr. Hogan?" We climbed on the rock and Grampa put his arm around me as we soared off into space, flying first over Lake Tioga, then back over the village with its tiny houses so far below. Grampa kept up a running commentary all the way and soon I was doing it too. Finally we flew back to Mount Baldy in a big circle. "Now, Boy," Grampa roared, "We're a coming down, so hold tight. And keep your head up high. Boy. It may be a rough landing."

I remembered those words once when many years later I was on a plane going to Nashville to make a speech. Over the intercom came the Captain's voice. "Folks," he said cheerily. "We're having a little problem getting the landing gear down. The co-pilot with the help of one of you strong men will try to auger it down manually." The co-pilot appeared with a large device looking like a brace and bit and he and one of the passengers tried in vain to turn it. "I guess, folks, that we'll have to skip Nashville this time and go on to Atlanta for our belly landing. They have better foam and firefighting equipment and a longer runway. We'll make it."

At Atlanta we circled around and around for a long time, ditching fuel, before he told us to put our heads between our knees and against the seat in front of us and to remember where the exits were. How deathly silent that plane was except for the murmur of people praying. Crouched in that fetal position, I remembered Grampa's command to hold my head high and when I did so, I felt a lot better. If I were going to die, I'd die proud, not craven. Ride 'em cowboy! The plane came down with a crash and skidded in sparks and foam almost to the end of the runway. Thanks to Grampa, I felt proud of myself even though I had a sore neck for a week afterwards.

Among the many things Grampa taught me was to know and appreciate many of the facets of that jewel, the Upper Peninsula of Michigan. Each of our "ex-pe-dit-ions" (He always sounded out big words) was a journey of discovery. Let me give you just one example. One morning Grampa was carrying a little pail when we set out for our walk, first through the Grove, then through Company Field, and finally down to the big beaver dam swamp. "No, Mr. McGillicuddy," he said when I asked him if the pail was for coffee. "I'm all out of shaving lotion so I thought I'd brew up a batch of my own, if you will kindly help me, sir, to pro-cure some of the in-gre-dients." He gave me a bag to hold them.

That whole morning was a delight. Tips of balsam fir which we squeezed and sniffed were the first to go in the bag, then some sassafrass bark. Grampa apologized to the bush for slicing the strip and gave me some to chew. Then we found some sweet grass, the kind Pete Half Shoes used in the aromatic baskets he occasionally wove. In the field we also plucked some sour-sap, a weed with a tangy taste almost like vinegar. Down by the Beaver Dam we found wintergreen berries, wild mint and Labrador tea leaves. Grampa picked a big leaf of skunk cabbage and asked me my opinion as to its suitablity before throwing it away and washing his hands in the creek. Lord, we must have smelled and tasted fifty kinds of bark and leaves before he said, "There's only one more thing we need for our con-coc-tion, Mr. McGillicuddy - some witch hazel." Finally we found that bush and Grampa and I picked a lot of little flowers off the tips of its branches. We boiled the stuff in a pail over the campfire and next morning anointed ourselves with it.

Day after day we went on other expeditions, all of which opened my eyes and ears and mind to the wonders of the U.P. One time we went on an orn-i-tho-logical expedition, collecting birds or rather writing their names down. Grampa Gage knew his birds and taught me all he knew - and a bit more. For example, once he stopped suddenly and held up a finger. "Hear that gurgle, Mr. Grogan? Over there in those pine trees." I listened hard but couldn't hear anything but the wind in their branches. "There it is again," he said. "That's a double-breasted drib. Very rare. It's the only bird that flies backwards to see where it's been." Hey, only now as I type this do I realize that drib is bird spelled backwards. Oh Grampa, you lovely crazy old bugger! But I've been a bird watcher ever since, to the enrichment of my days.

One day when we went trout fishing the flies were terrible: mosquitoes, black flies, deer flies, gnats and no-see-ums. It also was very warm and the sweat poured off our faces while not a trout rose to our flies. Suddenly Grampa let out a yell. "Enough!" he hollered. "Boy! Remember this: We don't have to endure the unbearable. Let's get the hell out!" We did! And that command got me into trouble in Australia. Let me explain.

When I became thirty I made a life plan for myself. During my thirties I would explore new human relationships. I did. I got married. My forties I would spend in creativity. I did. I fathered three fine children and wrote ten textbooks in the new field of speech therapy. My fifties I would spend in becoming wise; my sixties in folly; and my seventies in becoming resigned. The only trouble was that in my fifties my new found wisdom made it clear that if I postponed my follies for ten more years I probably wouldn't be able to enjoy them so I switched and made that decade my age of foolishness. I soon discovered that the basic prescription for folly was just to say yes.

Thus it was that when someone called me from New York and asked me if I would go as this country's representative in speech therapy to a Pan Pacific Conference on the Disabled in Sidney, Australia, all expenses paid, I said yes immediately and automatically. I didn't want to go to Australia but these were my years of folly so I said yes.

So after a gruelling eighteen hour flight in a propellor driven plane from San Francisco via Hawaii and the Fiji Islands I found myself completely exhausted in the Hotel Australia. Shortly after I'd gone to bed the phone rang. "I am Joyce Johnson, your hostess," she said in a stiff very British accent. There will be a reception for all the delegates to the conference at the governor's palace this evening at eight and I will be in the lobby to take you there at that time."

I tried to beg off but she wouldn't hear of it. Thus it was that I, a child of Lake Superior and its forests, under the tutelage of Miss Joyce, became a part of a crowd of people milling around in the huge reception hall under the chandeliers, making polite conversation that no one could hear, and nursing champagne and hors d'ouvres proferred endlessly by butlers or such. After the first hour of making fake faces and small nonsense talk, I was in a daze. After two hours of the hullabaloo I remembered Grampa's words: "You don't have to endure the unbearable. Get the hell out!"

When I told Miss Joyce I was leaving, she had a polite British fit. "No," she said. "That's completely indefensible. We haven't even gone through the reception line yet. You just cahn't." But I did. I fled out of the door, crawled in one of the waiting cabs and told the driver to get me the hell out of there, to show me the seamy side of Sidney, its pubs, and famous beaches. A gay rascal and fine storyteller, the cabbie sure followed my instructions. But Miss Joyce Johnson never forgave me.

One afternoon Grandpa found me encircling items in a Sears Roebuck catalog. "Why are you doing that?" he asked. I told him that I was picking out all the things I would buy when I grew up and had a lot of money. "Fool!" he roared. "The more stuff you buy, the poorer you are." And then he took me down to Lake Tioga, gave me a five dollar gold piece, and insisted I throw it way out into the lake. "The only nice thing about having money is that you can despise it," he said. "And the more possessions you have, the more they possess you." I learned a lot from Grampa Gage.

On another expedition when we were collecting "rep-tiles" I spied a toad but wouldn't pick it up, fearing that I'd get warts from the ugly creature. "Nonsense!" exclaimed Grampa. Then he told me the story of the prince who had been turned into a toad by a sorcerer and how he stayed a toad until kissed by a beautiful maiden. "Let's see if we can make a princess out of this one," he said. He picked up the toad, showed me the beautiful jewel that was its eye, then kissed it. Nothing happened but he taught me that, if you looked closely enough, nothing was really ugly.

I remember vividly one morning when I didn't get up to have Grampa shave me. It had rained hard for three days and was raining again. "Why get up?" I asked him when he came to my bedroom to see what was wrong. "Raining again. Another lousy day," I said as I pulled the covers over my head. Grampa pulled them back and marched me to the bathroom, then took my hand and put it inside his shirt.

"What does it feel like?" he demanded.

"It feels warm," I replied.

Grandpa grinned. "Yes," he said. "You're feeling the sunshine inside my skin sack. It's not the weather outside but the weather inside that counts. Now let's go down and have some breakfast."

I've remembered those words often in my long life and always felt better because I did. Once when I was in Ireland I made arrangements to go flyfishing for trout on one of their lovely lakes but when my ghillie (guide) called for me at six thirty in the morning I almost backed out. A nasty day, cold, and drizzling. I put a bottle of whiskey in my coat to make sure I'd have some of Grampa's sunshine in my skin sack.

Paddy McMullan, my ghillie, was a very old man, bewhiskered and disreputable, and the old Ford he drove was almost as old as he was. We rattled along a bumpy back road to the ruins of an ancient castle at the edge of a large lake. The boat, hidden in the bushes, leaked. The ancient bamboo flyrod was heavy and stiff but I finally was able to master it enough to make some good casts.

"Begging yer pardon, sorr," Paddy said. "You'll niver catch an Irish trout that way - except in a river. You have to dap, not let the fly sit on the water. I'll show ye." Paddy was a master fly fisherman and caught a trout on his first dap. The moment the fly hit the water, he'd quickly retrieve it, then flick it out again, over and over again, sometimes skittering the fly along a foot of the surface thereby creating the illusion of a hatch. Very difficult to do, it took me some time before I got the hang of it and to celebrate the accomplishment I brought out the bottle of whiskey. The old man's rheumy eyes sure lit up when he saw that bottle and he took a huge swallow from it.

I swear that Paddy knew where every fish was in that lovely lake. He'd row me over to a patch of reeds and say, "Ah, there's a good one here, sorr." And there almost always was. At each new location Paddy usually tied on a new trout fly. About midmorning the action slowed down: "May I have that bottle. sorr?" the old man asked. When I gave it to him, Paddy dipped a new fly in the whiskey, handed me the rod, and said. "Here's one for the gintlman! We Irish like whiskey, that we do, trout or man." As I cast, I noticed out of the corner of my eye that he took a big gulp from the brown bottle. Again I began to catch trout, Paddy dipping the fly in the whiskey and sneaking a snort of it with each cast. Perhaps I managed to get two or three swallows of liquid sunshine before the bottle was empty but no matter. Thanks to Grampa and Paddy McMullan it was one of the best mornings of my life.

On another occasion Grampa and I went hunting for gold in the granite hills north of Tioga. We didn't find any though once after he had distracted me by asking me to look over there at a pileated peewee I found a silver dollar where I had been digging. What I remember most about that trip though was what happened on our way back. Suddenly I got so utterly fatigued I couldn't stand up let alone walk any more. Grandpa was both concerned and sympathetic. "You old fool," he said to himself. "You forget the boy is only nine." Finally, after I'd lain in the grass a long time with him sitting beside me, he said, "Well, Mr. O'Connor, it's time for us to be hiking home again."

I began to cry. "I can't, Grampa," I wailed. "I'm too tired to move."

He stood me up then gave me a little talk about how all of us have a tank of reserve strength within us that we can use when all our other strength is gone. "I shall now turn on that tank, Boy," he said as he turned his finger in my navel. "Now forward march! You're a member of Sousa's famous band." Then he sang a song I'd never heard before, one that set me laughing, and down the path we went strutting like drum majors. Here's his song and the tune was that of one of Sousa's marches:

Do yer balls hang high? Do yer balls hang low?

Can you tie 'em in a knot? Can you tie 'em in a bow?

Can you throw them o'er yer shoulder like a European soldier?

Do yer balls hang low?

There have been several times in my life when I had to call upon that tank of reserve strength behind my navel. Once was when my heart stopped as my wife was driving me to the Emergency room of our hospital but another came when I'd shot a goose on a little muskeg lake near my cabin at Bitely. It was almost dark and the dead goose was floating about ten feet from the edge of the matted muskeg. I knew better but this was in my decade of folly so, leaving my gun on the shore, I picked up a pole and tiptoed my way out on that swaying muskeg, hoping to be able to bring the goose within reach. Suddenly all the matted growth gave way and into the icy water I went. There was no solid bottom, just ooze, and my soaked heavy clothing so weighted me down that swimming was almost impossible. No one knew where I was. After struggling in the muck for some time I became exhausted and almost gave up until I remembered Grandpa's insistence that I owned a tank of reserve strength. So I turned it on and finally managed to make my way to solid ground. I still don't know how I ever was able to do it.

But the most important thing that Grandpa Gage ever said to me was the word "Enjoy!" Let me tell you about it. We had walked the two miles down the old railroad track to the bridge, really a trestle, high above the Escanaba, a tributary of the Tioga River. When we got there, I began to cross on my hands and knees, always having had the fear of heights and those spaces between the railroad ties looked very big. Grandpa was outraged. "Walk like a man!" he commanded but I couldn't do it. It had rained earlier that morning and the ties were still wet but Grandpa began to skip across the outside edge of the ties to show me I had nothing to fear. Alas, he slipped and fell into the big pool below the bridge but not until I heard him shout, still in mid-air and before the splash, "Enjoy! Enjoy!" He came up snorting and escorted me across the bridge hand in hand and skipping too. I have never forgotten that admonition. "Enjoy! Enjoy!" has been the mandate of my days. I hope it will be yours, too.

THE STRAP

This is an account of how Fisheye stole Old Blue Balls' strap and the consequences thereof. But first, so that you can understand, let me forsake my usual happy nostalgia about my homeland, the Upper Peninsula of Michigan in the early days of this century, to give another side of the picture. It was a hard, harsh land, very primitive, first settled only a few decades earlier by miners, loggers or a few farmers, most of them immigrants from countries over the seas.

The climate was fierce, especially in the winter, the long winter from October until May, when the winds blew down from Lake Superior to bury the countryside in huge drifts of snow. For months on end the temperature was always below zero, sometimes as bitter as forty or fifty below. There were a few summers when frost occurred every month, and a lot of them when terrible thunderstorms crashed their lightning bolts all about us day or night. Forest fires swept through the slashings, filling our little village of Tioga with so much smoke it was hard to breathe.

Above all, there was always that feeling of isolation from the rest of the world. No radio, no TV, no real roads between towns, just two wagon ruts. No automobiles or planes. Only four people in Tioga got newspapers and these were passed on from family to family until they were shredded or plastered against the inside walls of the cabins to keep out the wind. Only the railroads linked us with the outside world and tickets cost biting money to get away.

Tioga was our world, our tiny world.

Hard lands breed or make hard people. Ours had to be tough to survive. Our men in the mines worked ten or twelve hour shifts for a dollar a day, came home to eat and fall asleep, and then spent their Sundays fishing, hunting for food, or making hay and wood for the winter to come. It was dangerous work. I recall Henry Thompson, our mining superintendent telling my father that he had to go to Duluth to catch hell from headquarters because seven men had already died that year, two more than the quota allowed. "They don't give a damn about the men," Thompson said, "but they'd budgeted for only five for the year and there are still two months to go." Many others got maimed or crippled. No one sued the mining companies because all the local lawyers had accepted retainer fees from them. If the families got a hundred dollars in death benefits and a tiny pension, they felt lucky. At least they could keep their houses or cabins unless they caused trouble because all the land was owned by the mining company. Eviction without mercy was swift and sure. It was hard to save money because again the company owned the store, charged high prices and gave credit, so any paycheck didn't last long. Most of our miners stayed in debt all their working lives.

The logging business was equally dangerous. No, not quite, but men were killed every year in the woods. When a tree is felled but lodges its branches in a nearby tree, it is still called a "widow-maker" in the U.P. Some trees when almost sawed through suddenly "kick back" wiping out the men who are sawing. Loading the huge logs on sleighs or railroad cars, riding the logs on the river drive took their toll of human lives and led to many personal tragedies. A harsh life and a very dangerous one.

Our women had to be tough too. They bore many children not just because sex is the poetry of the poor but so the family could have cheap labor until the kids grew up and went away and perhaps because they might have one of them who could tend them in their old age. Our women were always tired. They milked the cows and churned the butter. They tended the garden, did the interminable washings with nothing but a blue faced scrubbing board and the sad irons heated on the kitchen woodstove. They did the baking and canning and cooking, hauled the water from the well, read their bibles and prayed. Prayed to a cruel and fearful God not only for forgiveness from their current little sinnings but for the original sin bequeathed to them at birth from Adam and Eve. Every Sunday they were reminded of the hell and brimstone and damnation that might await them in the hereafter.

Like the sound made by the rat that gnaws at the cellar steps at night, fears gnawed at their lives, fear that the woodpile or the cans of berries and venison would run out, fear that the well would run dry, fear of the always encroaching forest, fears of illness or accidents, fear of losing one's job. No, the good old days weren't all that good.

When fear and danger and drudgery are mixed together the resulting brew has anger in it. There was a lot of brutality in our lives. The camp boss ruled his men with his fists. You did what he said without protest or complaining or he knocked you down. The mining captain was king and the foremen down to the straw bosses had absolute power. No one ever argued with the man above him.

In turn, the father was king of his cabin too. His word was law; you disobeyed at your peril. Punishment was swift and very harsh, even brutal. I recall once driving with my father as he made house calls on some patients down in French Town at the bottom of the hill and seeing a man beating a tied up horse. He was hitting it over and over again with a two-by-four with terribly hard blows. Awful!

When I asked my father why he didn't stop it, he said, "Cully, that's his business, not mine. If I'd gotten out of the buggy and protested he'd have hit me with that two-by-four too. Life is cruel, as you'll find out some day." I thought of some of the thrashings he'd given me and felt that I'd already found out. My father was a decent man but when he became furious with me for something I had or hadn't done, he beat me up pretty badly. I recall once refusing my mother's request that I take a bath because I knew she'd see the terrible purple bruises he'd given me. When I lost the argument and she did see them I just said I'd had a bad fight in school. I wasn't the only one who got thrashed severely by a father. All of my friends had too. We felt we had it coming. We also learned the art of taking a licking. You didn't shed any tears. Men and boys were never ever to cry. You just yelped loudly after each blow until they stopped, and then you could go off by yourself and weep. Spare the rod and spoil the child. There weren't many spoiled boys in Tioga.

Our schools of course reflected the cultural practices of the time. Along with blackboards each room was furnished with birch switches, often well worn with the white bark long gone. Only in first and fourth grades had they never been used, the grades taught by Margaret and Nellie Feeley whom we loved too much to cause any trouble. By the time we were in the sixth grade most of us were too big to switch (we just laughed defiantly if the teacher used the birch or we brought her some new bigger switches) so for serious infractions we were sent up to Old Blue Balls' office.

That was big trouble! Mr. Donegal, Old Blue Balls as we called him behind his back, was a disciplinarian of the old school. A short but powerful man, he ruled our school by fear. Not only us kids but all of the teachers were terrified of him and with good reason. He would invade our classrooms, watch the teaching and criticize it, or take over the teaching himself. He patrolled the hallways and schoolyard, sometimes actually hauling a boy by his hair up to his dreaded office. Old Blue Balls would even go to a boy's home if he suspected the latter was playing hookey and look under the bed. And his bite was worse than his bark, which is saying a lot.

Mr. Donegal had three favorite methods of corporal punishment - the ruler across the wrists for minor devilment, THE HAND, (we always capitalized it), and The Strap. Most of us who had known all three claimed that The Strap was the worst. Old Blue Balls would have you get on all fours on his office floor, then whop you as many hard ones as he deemed you deserved, then, after a pause, one terribly hard one so you'd never, never do it again. It sure was difficult to sit down after you'd had The Strap. I remember doing my duty under a bush rather than sit on the outhouse hole.

Mr. Donegal had ruled his school long enough that there were in it children whose fathers he had thrashed in their time. But times were changing. Almost unheard of earlier, parents began to complain to my father, who was also secretary of the school board, that Old Blue Balls' punishments were too severe, that as he had grown older he had become more brutal. But, because my father and Mr. Donegal were the closest of friends and hunting and fishing partners, he never mentioned it to his friend. "Whatever his methods, he runs a fine school," my father told them, "the best one in the county. We have more students going on to college than from any school around. They're getting a fine education."

One autumn afternoon just before school was to be dismissed my close friend Fisheye dipped Amy Erickson's pigtails that hung over his desk into his inkwell, turning the ends of those pigtails from blonde to black brunette. She had it coming. She'd been teasing him about his broken shoes which were all he had. One of our unwritten laws was the boys shouldn't hit girls no matter what the provocation so he had to get even somehow. Well, Amy tattled and raised cain and our teacher sent Fisheye up to Old Blue Balls' office with a note explaining what had happened.

But Mr. Donegal had sneaked out early so he could go partridge hunting and Fisheye waited and waited until finally he said to hell with it, and left the school himself. But not before he stole THE STRAP. He'd been looking at it for sometime with dread even though he knew it well, and on an impulse at the last moment he just tucked it under his shirt and ran down the stairs. The ultimate crime, the great revenge! God knows what Old Blue Balls would do if he found out who had swiped it! At the moment Fisheye didn't care. He felt ten feet tall.

Of course he had to share The Strap with us after swearing us to secrecy, Mullu and me, anyway. It was the trophy of trophies but not one to parade around so we hung it from the roof of a decrepit little shack we'd built some time before in Beaver Dam Swamp. Better than a set of deer antlers, it was. We used to take it down to feel it and give each other a few light licks, then run around bellowing. Fisheye was our hero. He had chopped off our dragon's tail. Afternoon after afternoon we went down to that shack to admire The Strap, tell tales about the lickings we'd had, and eat slices of raw potato with salt or sticks of rhubarb with sugar.

Somehow Old Blue Balls never discovered who had stolen his strap but that didn't phase him in the slightest. What he did was to get some ironwood shoots about four feet long and about an inch thick at the base. Now ironwood is the toughest wood in the whole U.P., almost impossible to cut with a knife. We kids used to make bows of it for our arrows and it was always hard to bend, even after we peeled off its black wrinkled bark. Mullu was the first of our trio to get trimmed by Old Blue Balls with those ironwood shoots and when we saw his behind we were scared crazy. Great purple and black welts ran across his butt and his back at least a quarter of an inch wide. Some bleeding too. No licking we'd ever had had looked like that. The ruler was bad enough; THE HAND was worse; The Strap was awful but none of them left their mark on the flesh as deeply as did those ironwood shoots. We sure resolved to be on our best behavior. When another kid, a grade beyond ours, suffered the same thrashing and wasn't able to come back to school for two days, we held a pow wow down at our shack and decided that Fisheve should somehow return The Strap to Old Blue Balls' office. I don't know how he managed it but he did for I saw it hanging in its familiar place on the desk. I also saw the group of black ironwood sticks. No, I didn't get thrashed that time; I just had to take a message from our teacher. I think she just wanted some extra chalk, but I saw those sticks and wanted no part of them. Of course the whole school heard of them too and for some time there were few disciplinary problems.

But boys will be hellions when the urge comes over them and Sulu made the mistake of hitting the teacher with a short strip of rubber band. They could really hurt if you fastened one end over a sharp pencil, aimed it right, pulled it back and then let go. Sulu's aim was accurate and he hit her right behind the ear. Sure made her holler! Now that, of course, was a major infraction so Old Blue Balls again passed by The Strap for the ironwood sticks.

That evening after supper Sulu's father came down to Mr. Donegal's house carrying a black stick which he placed on the railing of the porch before knocking at the door. "Won't you please come in?" Mrs. Donegal asked. "No, I'd like to talk to your husband out here," Sulu's father replied.

When Mr. Donegal came onto his porch he failed to notice the grey-white look on Sulu's father's face. Finns rarely show much emotion but when their faces turn that color they are furious and you'd better watch out.

"What can I do for you?" asked Mr. Donegal. "You interrupted my supper."

Fighting down his anger, Sulu's father began slowly and carefully. "You beat my boy, Sulu, today pretty bad but I make you a bargain. If he do bad things, you tell me and I punish, not you. You hurt him bad."

Old Blue Balls was enraged. No one had ever challenged his authority before. He put his face close to Sulu's father's and roared, "I'll have you know that I run my school the way it ought to be run. When you were a boy I had to punish you. No to your bargain! No, no, no! If Sulu was dumb enough to hit one of our teachers with a rubber band, he got what he had coming, and if he does it again he'll get it worse."

Sulu's father pole-axed old Blue Balls right there on the porch with a right upper-cut to the jaw. And then he took that black ironwood cane and beat the prone superintendent again and again on his back and hindend as hard as he could. Then he placed the ironwood cane against the porch railing and left.

When Mr. Donegal recovered enough to go to my father for help, Dad put ointment on his welts and a bit of bandage on cuts. "You've sure taken a hard beating, Fred," he said. "how did it happen?"

Our superintendent told him the whole story, even about the ironwood canes, and swore that next morning he'd press charges for assault and battery and have the bastard put in jail.

"Well," said Dad. "Perhaps you can make a case for yourself if the prosecuter down in Marquette would agree, which might not be certain if he sees Sulu's back. Fred, I hate to say it, for we've been friends for so many years and had such good companionship which I would miss greatly, but don't you think it's about time you retire? Times have changed. I've had a lot of complaints from our people about your brutality and cruelty and have protected you because of our friendship. Go to bed for two days and think it over." My father always told it straight. I remember him telling a man, "Pete, you have at most only six months to live. Make the most of them." Mr. Donegal said he'd go to bed and think it over.

And he did retire. He went back to the family farm in Indiana and raised canteloups and watermelons until he died. All that just because Fisheye stole The Strap!

LICE AREN'T NICE

John," my mother asked, "Will you look at my scalp? It's been itching a lot lately. I suppose it's just the usual lack of humidity that always comes in January when the house has been closed so long. I'll pobably have to put some steaming teakettles on all the stoves."

Dad looked her over. "No, Edyth," he said. "You've got head lice. See, here's a big grayback." He plucked it off her collar before knicking it with his thumbnail.

"No! No! Oh dear no! Don't tell me!" She was almost in tears.

Dad had been prowling around in her hair. "Yes, Edyth," he replied. "Your hair is full of them, and a lot of nits too. Nits are their eggs. Can happen to anyone up in this country especially in the winter. Well, I'll go over to the dispensary and bring back some oil of myrrh so you can rub it in before and after you wash your hair. Have you one of those fine tooth combs, the kind you used on Cully about three years ago when he got lousy?" She nodded. "If you use the myrrh and comb hard and long, you'll get the nits. They're little gray or white things, almost specks. May take a week of combing and washing your hair before they're gone. And don't scratch! No use getting a scalp infection too. I also suggest that you put a heavy towel around your neck to catch those that fall out when you comb, and to wipe the comb with. Then put it outside in the snow so they'll freeze to death."

When Dad returned from the hospital, Mother already had her hair down and a towel around her neck. He poured some of the oil of myrrh in a saucer and put the bottle beside it. "Now be sure to comb hard right near the scalp," he said. "That's where the little buggers hang out. And if you find any lice or nits on the comb put it in the basin before you wipe it on the towel. And, before you begin, take a look at my scalp. I suppose I'm getting them too."

Mother looked hard but couldn't find any. "Oh, I've just got too tough a skin," my father said. "Smoking Granger tobacco in my pipes keeps the insects away. Mosquitoes don't bother me, as you know, and probably lice don't like the flavor. If I were a louse I'd prefer your pretty head to mine anytime. Anyway, it's no great catastrophe. As David Harum said, "A certain amount of fleas is good for a dog; it keeps him from brooding on being a dog." Mother almost threw the bottle at him. As he left, he asked to be sure to check the boys' heads when they got back from school. "And Dorothy's too," he said. "Even if she's not old enough yet to go to school, you might have given some of yours to her."

That afternoon Dad was holding his office hours in the old hospital across the street when Fred Donegal, our tough school superintendent, the one we kids called Old Blue Balls, came to see him. "Doctor," he said, "I'm afraid the school's coming down with an epidemic of head lice and I'd like your advice about what to do. Odd thing, though, only the kindergarten, the second grade, and the fifth grade kids are lousy, and of course not all of them are. Can't figure out why only those grades are infested, but I know that soon all of them will be."

"Yes," said my father. "Head lice sure can spread fast. Haven't had an epidemic for three years now so I suppose it was bound to come. Some father probably came back from a lumber camp and gave them to his kids. I suggest that you tell all your teachers to keep in from recess any kid who's scratching his head, look him over and send him home if he has lice. It's hard to understand, though, why the outbreak is confined to just those grades."

"How do you treat an infestation of head lice?" Mr. Donegal asked. "What should I tell them to do?"

"The Finns have an old remedy," my father replied. "They either shave off or clip off all the hair on the head or soak the scalp with kerosene. Others just shave the scalps bare. That works though the kids will have some pretty cold heads in this winter weather, and the girls won't stand for it."

"But the kerosene?"

"Yes," my father replied. "Rubbing kerosene in the scalp will get rid of the lice and some of the nits but it burns the scalp. The best treatment is oil of myrrh and hard combing. I fear many will feel they can't afford the myrrh. I have a quart of it and you can tell them I'll give them a bottle of myrrh free until it's all gone. May stink up your schoolrooms. And be sure to tell them to comb hard with a fine tooth comb so they can get the nits. I just hope they have one or that they can get one up at Flynn's store."

"Will going to the sauna do any good, Doctor, "Mr. Donegal asked.

"Those head lice are tough," my father answered. "I doubt it. I've heard tell that some of the old Finns first go to the sauna, then wet their heads, and roll in the snowbank afterwards to get rid of them. One Finn told me once that he got rid of his lice by rubbing his dog over his head. I doubt that too. Human lice prefer human heads just as chicken lice prefer feathers. Probably all that really happened was that he added some dog fleas which are not so particular."

When Dad got home he asked if any of us had lice. "No," my mother said. I've gone over their heads with the fine toothed comb thoroughly and didn't find a single nit nor louse. John, how did I get them?" she wailed. "I haven't been out of the house for weeks except to go to church and then I keep my hat on like the other women do, although I think it's silly."

"Well I don't know where you got them either," Dad replied. There's a good chance the two boys will be getting them later." He told her about Mr. Donegal's conversation. "Cully in the fifth grade and Joe is in kindergarten two of the three grades where they've appeared. You be sure to check them every day."

Mother sure did. I got so I almost hated to get up in the morning because I got combed before breakfast, again when I came from school at noon, and again before supper. This went on day after day even though she never found a louse or nit. Then one afternoon before supper she found two. I knew what had happened. Fisheye and I were the only boys in our grade that still had hair. All the others had heads that were clipped or shaved. And we'd been wrestling. Well, finding those two lice sure raised cain. Mother redoubled her efforts, scraping my scalp rather then just combing, and rubbing that stinky myrrh stuff all over my head. Oh how I hated the smell of it, not only on me but even on her, for she was still using it as well as combing and washing her own hair daily. Each morning before I went to school I had to fill the big copper boiler with packed snow so she could have soft water to do her hair. The water from our well was full of iron and left orange stains on the sink that only Zud could remove. In the summer she used soft water from the rain barrel outside under the eaves but only melted snow could provide it in January.

I just couldn't understand why she was making such a big deal of a few pesky lice. My head wasn't itching even if it was sore from the combing. "Lice aren't nice," she told me. "A louse in the house is almost as bad as having bedbugs." Oh how she battled them, boiling the brushes and combs, scouring the hats and caps with wood alcohol, then putting them outside to freeze. Twice a day she ran the carpet sweeper not only over the floor but even on the upholstered chairs and couch. I sure got tired of having her examine the collar of my jackets or sweaters and always parting and peering at my hair.

Finally, at school I was the only boy with hair, Fisheye's uncle having shaved his head so close he was bald as an onion. How the schoolroom stank of kerosene and myrrh so I decided I'd have my head shaved too. When I brought the subject up to mother, she vetoed it immediately. "No, you don't, Cully. You have such nice thick hair like your father. I don't want you looking like a convict in prison."

But I was determined. If I got my head shaved there'd be no more combing agony two or three times a day and besides I didn't want to be different from the other boys. So one afternoon after school I went upstairs to my bedroom and tried to open my piggy bank to get money for the barber, Mr. Rich. It really wasn't a piggy bank. It looked like a little banker sitting in a cast iron chair. When you lifted up his iron arm and put a coin in the hand, the arm would come down and slip the coin into the banker's pocket. Real neat! It worked every time. But getting money out of that banker bank was hard going. Underneath the chair was the opening, covered by a plate that was screwed down so tight I just couldn't turn it. I had quite a lot of money in that bank, so much that it hardly rattled any more when you shook it. Yes, there were even two ten dollar gold pieces in it that my beloved Grampa Gage had given me. I sure wished he hadn't tightened that screw so tightly. Finally, by holding the bank upside down between my knees and turning the screwdriver with a pair of pliers, I got it open at last. Wow, what a pile of money there was! I was rich! Taking only a quarter for the haircut and a dime for candy, I put the rest of the coins back, replaced the plate and made sure not to tighten the screw too tight. Then I went to the barber shop.

When I told Mr. Rich that I wanted my head shaved, he said no, that he'd only shave it if I brought a note from my mother. He'd clip it short, though, if I wanted. So that's what I had him do. It was quite an ordeal. Mr. Rich was an ex-miner who had lost a leg in a mining accident and the wooden leg he wore often hurt him so he left it in a corner as he hopped around the barber chair. Since he chewed snuff, his heavy breath was full of that smell but his clippers were the worst. They were hand operated because we had no electricity back then and they were very dull, often yanking out the hair rather than cutting it. After what seemed like an eternity of torture, the barber turned the chair around so I could see what he had done. I hardly recognized myself. Paying him the quarter I then bought two strips of black licorice and went home to face my mother.

She wept when she saw me but the deed was done. She did insist on taking my picture as I held a piece of cardboard with the number 1729 on it and for a week she called me Convict 1729 instead of Cully. My father approved not only my head but my gumption but he also confiscated my bank. "When you want money ask me for it," he said. "A savings bank is to put money in not take out."

Well everything has an end and a woman has two, as my Grampa Gage often remarked. Finally my mother stopped scraping my scalp, the kerosene smell in school faded, and we no longer were afraid to scratch our heads. Even mother stopped smelling of myrrh. Dad told us why. "All epidemics are self limiting," he said. "Our people are generally a clean folk and can't abide lice. Besides, the life cycle of a louse is only thirty days from the first tiny nit to maturity and most adult lice only live three days. They can do a lot of blood sucking in that time and that's what makes the itch. Once you get rid of the eggs, the nits, the problem solves itself. I just wish I knew how this epidemic got started."

I think it was about the end of March when he found out. One evening after supper Dad was sitting in his Morris chair very content. He'd had venison chops, mashed potatoes, rutabagas, and blueberry pie with a piece of store cheese and he had read the Chicago Tribune. I hovered around knowing that this was the time he tended to share with my mother accounts of his practice. We kids weren't supposed to listen but I did, knowing well that if I ever told them to anyone else I would probably be beheaded. I'd heard a lot of dandy ones over the years like the one about the lumberjack who slashed his leg with an axe, got drunk, and lay in the sun for two days before they brought him to my father. "And you know what?" Dad would say. "When I squeezed that leg a whole procession of maggots promenaded out of the wound in single file. And that wound was clean as a whistle. No pus, no proud flesh, no nothing. All I had to do was put in a few stitches. We ought to have flies and maggots in our pharmacopeia."

But on this particular night, Dad wasn't telling any tales. Instead, he said to mother, "You know, Edyth, medicine is not only an art but a science. A scientist knows that there is always a solution to any problem; he abhors unknowns. Well, I've been troubled for more than a month trying to figure out how our louse epidemic got started. The essential facts are these: you and the kindergarten, second grade and fifth grade kids all came down with lice at the same time. What then could be the common source? It must have been their teachers. Now I vaguely recall that you had those teachers here for tea one Saturday afternoon early in January, had a hilarious time, and then went up to Flynn's store. Well, I went up to Flynn's store too this afternoon and looked at some of those silly women's hats Flynn has had up there for years.

"Oh no," mother moaned. "Of course that's where we got the lice. The four of us had a lark trying on those crazy hats. Of course, that's what happened. Oh dear, we started all this trouble."

"Looks like you did," said my father. "Anyway, when I looked inside those hats I found plenty of lice so I bought the whole batch of them for five dollars and brought them home. I thought you might like to try them on again."

"John, you didn't!" mother screamed. "Where are they? Where are they?"

Dad grinned. "I burned them up in the burning barrel."

U. P. CUSSING

At the beginning of this century the U.P. was a rough crude land. Its men were a hard working, hard fighting, hard drinking lot. In that harsh environment they almost had to be. Their speech was rough too; they were a hard cussing crew.

My first experience with profanity came when I was an innocent four year old. It was Sunday morning and, watching the people going to church, I saw Mr. Koski, clad in his very best Sunday suit, slip on a cow pasty (which is what we called those circular platters of manure), and sit down right in the middle of it. As he picked himself up and started back home he gave vent to some angry cussing, repeating it over and over again until he was out of sight.

Somehow his words had a good ring to them and so it was that my horrified mother found me marching around our dining room table chanting over and over again:

"Sonza bits,
Sonza bits,
Sonza, sonza, Sonzabits."

Emerging from the kitchen a moment later with a cake of Fels Naphtha soap in one hand and a wet washcloth in the other, she bade me stick out my tongue which she then anointed. When I began to cry, she took me on her lap, wiped away my tears, and gave me a little talking-to.

"Now Cully," she said. "I put that soap on your tongue so you would remember that we Gages do not swear nor talk dirty. I know you'll hear a lot of bad lanuage before you grow up but it isn't nice to talk that way, and I don't want you to curse and swear and use dirty words. You'll never hear me doing it, nor your father either. Please don't ever do it again!!"

What she said about my father was true. All the time I was growing up I never heard a bit of profanity come from his lips. Except once! When I was fifteen my father, and his crony, Jim Olson, took me with them on a trout fishing trip. To escape the mosquitoes we made our night fire on a bald granite hill above Brown's Dam. On one side of the fire was some thick moss and grass; on the other was just bare rock. They put their blankets on the moss while I was given the rock for a mattress. Fair enough! A boy knew his place. Men first!

Well, suddenly all hell broke loose. My father and Jim began to yell and swear, tearing off their clothes, dancing around and swatting themselves. They had bedded down on a red ant's nest. I pulled the blanket over my head to stifle my laughter but I recall vividly the torrent of cussing my father emitted. Never repeated himself once. I had to admire his repertoire. Later, when he was in his nineties and I reminded him of the experience, he laughed. "Yes, Cully. I haven't sworn very much ever since your mother made me promise, while I was courting her, that I'd break myself of swearing, drinking, and chewing tobacco, three nasty habits I'd contracted in Medical School. Well, as you know, I don't mind taking a nip or two on occasion but I did give up swearing and chewing tobacco. I started chewing tobacco when I was in Medical School and had to dissect cadavers. For some reason I've never been able to tolerate the smell of formaldehyde. Chewing tobacco took some of the stench out of my nose and mouth. The other students could go to the cold room, take a cadaver off the hook and dance her to the dissecting table, singing, "Waltz me around, Mamie; Waltz me around," but I never could because of the smell. So I backslid on only one of the three promises. Not bad!"

The almost universal proclivity to swearing is one that has existed since earliest times. My mother also swore, although I'm sure she never knew she did. When the cake collapsed in the oven as she tested it with a toothpick, she said, "Oh Drat!" the equivalent of "Oh Damn!" When the hired girl dropped and broke one of her Haviland china cups she said, "Oh, Dear! Oh, Dear Me!" When the knitting slipped off her needle in a tangle, she said "Fiddlesticks!" with an intonation that meant "Dammit to hell!" My mother never took the name of the Lord in vain and never uttered a dirty word but she did her share of cussing too.

I never heard my Grandma Gage do any cussing. She didn't need to, her tongue being razor sharp, as my beloved Grandpa Gage knew all his married days. "Arza," she would say. "You're as stupid as a newborn louse!" She, like my mother, was a Lady. My Grandma Van, on the other hand, was not. She was just a sweet old woman but when she forgot where she had hidden her false teeth or Civil War pension check (They were always under her pillow!) she would say "Scats!" and "Dang it!" Or call someone she didn't like a "danged copperhead!"

If I recall correctly, most of the swearing in Tioga was done by the men, not the women. Nevertheless, upon real provocation, the women would cuss too. We had only one German family in Tioga, the Rhinelanders, and I often played with their son, Fritz. Mrs. Rhinelander was a huge, powerful woman who beat up her husband and son. Once, when I was playing in their kitchen with Fritz, a cat jumped up on the table, whereupon Mrs. Rhinelander swept it off with a heavy blow, and with it a glass spoon holder that broke into many pieces. Fritz fled and I with him but not before I heard her exclaim, "Donder und Blitzen!" I put that in my collection.

Fisheye's mother and father were French Canadians and so their profane expressions were always in French. Once, when Fisheye's mother had just hung out a new washing, the clothes pole broke and the clean clothes sagged into the mud. "Nom de nom de, nom de chien!" she roared. That only meant "name of a dog," but it sure sounded like cursing. And was!

Mullu was Finnish and he taught me some of their choicest swear words. So did his mother one day when the cream she was churning just wouldn't turn into butter. "Saatana!" she said. Mrs. Salo also used that word when we put molasses around the hole of her outhouse. "Saatana! Saatana pelikeda!"

The most frequently used cusswords in Tioga were "hell" and, of course, "damn." The latter is an ancient word derived from the Latin "damnare" which means to injure or punish. It occurs at least 145 times in Shakespeare's plays and was spoken a thousand times each day in Tioga when I was a boy.

But not usually in anger! It usually meant "very." as in "That's a damned fine buck you got, Eino!" "You're still a damn good looking woman, Lempi," or "the best damn pasty I ever ate," "Yah, it's damned cold outside. Almost froze my bollix coming up the hill."

My friend Emerick tells a tale of his tough old Cornish grandfather who, on his wedding night, took off his pants and commanded his bride to put them on. "But they're too big for me," she protested. "Yes," the man replied, "and you better damned well never forget it, woman!"

The word hell was often used in the same way. "Hell no, Sulu. I no going to Polka with you in them clompers." Or, "That's a helluva big trout, Slimber. How in hell you snag him?" Or, "You did a helluva good job skinning that skunk, Arvo, but you sure stink like hell. Better go sauna!"

A lot of so-called swearing consists of exclamations rather than curses and the words *damn* and *hell* were often used in this sense. When Sven Olson was shingling his house, he put down the hammer to get some more nails from his pouch and inadvertently moved his hammer which fell to the ground. "Oh damn!" he exclaimed. "Oh hell! Oh Double hell!" He didn't mean to say anything profane. He was just venting his frustration which is a good thing. Or so we felt. When his neighbor, Felix De Forrest, was lowering a pail of butter, eggs and milk down his well to keep them cool on a warm summer's day and the rope broke we didn't condemn him for saying, "Mon Dieu! Oh hell and dammit!" Better to let the emotion out than keep it in.

Of course, there were times when the usual hells and damns were used as epithets, as curses, and so were a lot of other words. The appeals to the Deity for help in attacking other individuals or inanimate objects or even the curser himself were commonly heard. "God damn you, you so and so!" was not unusual nor was the appeal to the Virgin Mary from the French Canadians. The so-and-so's included a wide variety of vilifying phrases such as the sonovas: son of a bitch, of a whore, of a couchon (pig), of a gun! Oh there were many more that are unprintable. These were fighting words unless you said them with the preface "You old" and smiled as you said them. I remember thinking that a couple of lumberjacks were going to have a fight down at the railroad station because they were thumping each other and calling each other names but no, they had not seen each other for a long time and were just happy to meet again. "Ah Francoise, you Goddamn old bastard, where you been? Haven't seen you since we cleaned out that saloon at Big Bay!"

I never heard anyone ever commit blasphemy or curse God but I sure heard a lot of name-calling that occasionally included dirty words. Indeed name-calling was a part of the experience of growing up and I early learned to chant "Sticks and stones may break my bones but names will never hurt me!" But they did! Many of them included references to paternity: "You son of a pissant," "You son of a cur!" "You son of a skunk!" Others just described you in unpleasant terms: "You crooked, lop eared, dog-faced toad!" "You horse's ass! "You dog!" "You bag of snot!"

Some years ago I read a fat, scholarly book by Montagu entitled "The Anatomy of Swearing" which traced the history of the art from the Greeks and Egyptians to the present day. It listed all the four letter words (and others) that should never be spoken by civilized human beings, the words for intercourse, urination, defecation, and genitalia. They are well known so I don't have to put them down, remembering my mother's soap. However one of them, shit, should be mentioned because back then it did not seem vulgar at all. It was just the regularly used word for excrement, just another word, standard usage. It merely meant manure, and, Lord knows, there was plenty of it in Tioga where the cows and horses regularly roamed the streets and sidewalks. My mother never used it, being a lady, but she never said "manure" either. Her equivalent was the phrase "big dirty," as in "Did you do a big dirty, Cully?" Though casually used in our communication, the word was unpleasant enough to find its way into many of our profane expressions such as the Finnish "Buskan hosu" (shit pants!) or as an old Dutchman put it, "You're a big bag of skiet."

Another word that Montagu had on his list was the word "bloody!" Abhorred then in England as one of the dirtiest words in the language, it was brought to the U.P. by the Cornish miners along with their wonderful pasties and saffron bread. "You bloody bastard!" "You bloody bugger!" were common components in U.P. swearing, but, like shit, the word bloody was not felt to be unutterably vulgar.

For the most part, though, the bulk of U.P. cussing did not use these dirty words. They were reserved for situations involving extreme anger or frustration. I remember old man Trevarthan's swearing as he tried to split a big chunk of elm. Now elm has a diabolically twisted grain that grabs an axe and holds it stone-tight. If you put a wedge in the crack, that gets stuck too. Well, old man Trevarthan cursed for ten minutes straight before giving up and he never used a single really dirty word. It went something like this: "Damn my eyes if I won't chop you, you bloody bullheaded bugger, you dog, you blasted son of the swamp, Great balls of fire! Holy Hokey Pokey! Take that! and that! you crooked rotten devil" and so on.

It was said in Tioga that old man Marchand, our delivery man and mail carrier, owned the record for continuous swearing. It happened when he bought a new Model-T Ford without really learning how to drive it. He tried to steer it by yelling "Gee" and "Haw," as he did to his horses; he pulled up on the steering wheel shouting "Whoa!" when he wanted to stop; and he cursed that mechanical monster all the way up and down our steep hill street. Alas, he swore in French so I can't replicate it here but people who knew the language told me he never repeated himself. A two mile curse.

Pierre Trude was repairing the trim on the Catholic church with Father Hassel, our wise old priest, steadying the ladder, when he hit his thumb hard with the hammer. His face purpling, Pierre just mumbled something. Then he hit the thumb again. "Father," he said. "May I please use your outhouse?" "Of course, my son." When Pierre emerged, there was Father Hassel with the holy water. He knew the weaknesses of the flesh.

Yes, there was a lot of swearing done in the U.P. when I was a boy but most of it was pretty innocent, just an occasional damn or hell. There was little profanity or vulgarity, certainly not as much as I hear today. It never soared to artistic heights such as Shakespeare's: "The devil damn thee black, thou cream-faced loon. Where gottest thou that goose look?" Nor did it have the wit of the famous 18th century scholar, Dr. Samuel Johnson, who went down to a fishmarket to buy a fresh fish. Evidently he was pretty indecisive for the fishwife clerk called him every dirty name in the book. Dr. Johnson looked her in the eye. "And you, Madame, are a parallelogram!" Stopped her in her tracks! Yes, it isn't the words you use but how you say them that counts.

But I weary of my topic and, sensing a faint taste of Fels Naphtha in my mouth, I bring this little piece to a close with the song "Sammy Hall." When the old Cornish miner, Tim Squires, got snockered up sufficiently in Higley's saloon, and upon request, he would sing it loud and strong, with all the other customers joining in the chorus. And then he would sing it over and over again as he staggered up our hill street. I learned it by following him. Here we go!

Oh, my name is Sammy Hall, Sammy Hall, Sammy Hall,
Oh my name is Sammy Hall and I hate you one and all.
You're a gang of muckers all, Damn yer hide!

Oh I killed a man 'tis said, so 'tis said, so 'tis said.
Oh I killed a man, 'tis said, that I hit him on the head,
And I left him there for dead. Damn his hide!

To the gallows I must go. I must go. I must go.
To the gallows I must go with my friends all down below
Saying Sam, I told you so. Damn their hides!

Oh the preacher he did come; he did come; he did come.
Oh the preacher he did come and he looked so very glum
As he talked of kingdom come. Damn his hide!

Then Tim would shift to a falsetto as he sang the final verse:
There was Nellie in the crowd, in the crowd, in the crowd.
There was Nellie in the crowd, and she looked so very proud
That I told her right out loud: Damn yer hide!"

WIDOWS 'N ORPHANS

Old Man McGee had had a hard night. The heart pains had been bad, especially those where the elephant stepped on his chest, or so it felt. Hard to breathe. Oh, he'd taken several spoonsful of the medicine that Docter Gage had given him and they helped cut down the pains that rose up and ran down his arm but the old pump just wasn't working right. Kept stopping and then galloping. He'd sat up in the chair all night and was sure pooped when dawn came.

"Well, McGee," he said aloud to himself as he built a fire in the cookstove. "Might as well face it. Yer on yer last legs, McGee. You're gonna die, and damned near did last night. Just a matter of time."

The old man sure craved a cup of strong coffee but he was all out of coffee and wouldn't have any until his pension check came the end of the week. He dumped the coffee grounds from the blackened pot onto a plate. Naw, they were gray. He'd boiled them three days in a row and the last time it was just like drinking warm water. Of course he still had tea but somehow it's not too good in the morning when you need a bracer for the day. What his old gullet thirsted for was a mug of black java, strong enough to coat the fur of the tongue so you could taste it after the mug was empty. "Well, how about some swamp coffee?" the old man asked himself. "Just a snort of whiskey in enough hot water to soak the korpua so I kin chew it. Yea, that'll do, McGee. That'll do! But easy on the water, McGee! Easy on the water."

The old Scotsman felt better after breakfast but he was still thinking about dying. It had been a close call last night. No, he wasn't scared of dying but he did have some concern about what might happen in the hereafter. He knew it would be heaven or hell and the way the revivalist preachers painted the latter with fire and brimstone, McGee wanted no part of that.

"What are yer chances, McGee?" he asked aloud. "You ain't done any sinning to account for anything much since you were a young buck so that's in yer favor. But maybe St. Peter, he's kept track of them early doings. Got 'em down on a marble tablet, mebbe."

That worried the old man. Without his morning coffee it was hard to think straight but the thought came to him that maybe if he could do some good deeds he'd have a better chance of playing a golden harp on those heavenly stairs. "Yea, McGee. That's what you gotta do to cancel them early sinnings. Do some good deeds to widows 'n orphans, mebbe. Wasn't there something in the Bible about helping widowns 'n orphans?"

McGee knew his Bible, the one his old mother had given him when he left Scotland a million years ago. He read it every day. Widows and orphans and doing good deeds. Where would it be? Not in the first part, maybe in Psalms or Proverbs. These he thumbed through but found nothing except a lot of wisdom. Perhaps the New Testament would be a better bet. All morning he read Matthew, Mark, Luke and John without avail. Then he skipped to the apocrypra and by chance stumbled on I Esdras, II 20: "Do right to the widow, judge for the fatherless, give to the poor, defend the orphan, clothe the naked." Well, that wasn't just what he was hunting for but it would do. "Somehow, McGee," he said to himself. "You've got to do some good deeds for widows 'n orphans."

Unfortunately there weren't any orphans in Tioga. If other family members existed, they took the kids in. If not, then some other family did. For example, when Mr. and Mrs. Pelkie died of food poisoning from eating badly smoked fish at a neighbor's house leaving seven children ranging in age from two to twelve, they had all been adopted within three days, two of them by the neighbors who'd been deathly sick but recovered. In Tioga we took care of our own.

But there were some widow women, usually older ones who might need a man to do some things they found hard to do by themselves. Old man McGee could think of three right away who'd been without a man around the house for some time: Katy Flanagan, Helen Johnson, and Aunt Lizzie. Actually Katy Flanagan wasn't really a widow for she had a widely wandering husband who showed up every year or two for perhaps a week, then took off after he learned again he couldn't stand the rasp of her Irish tongue. But she might need help. Mrs. Johnson, a nice woman, had lost her husband only two years before. A logging accident. As for Aunt Lizzie, she'd had a lot of husbands who'd died on her but none recently.

After a lunch of bologna, cheese, hardtack and tea, McGee was so sleepy he lay in the bunk for a time, falling fast asleep and not awakening until almost dark. No time to do any good deeds and get stars in his crown until tomorrow. The old pump was thumping along nice and regular. "No, McGee," he said,

"You ain't going to die tonight. You kin start kerlecting your good deeds tomorrow."

The next morning McGee was feeling much better so after arming himself with a file, a hone, and an axe he started up our hill street. By the time he got to the Catholic Church he was out of breath so he rested a while on its steps. "Dang street!" old man McGee said. "Keeps tilting on me and getting steeper every year."

Soon, however, he was on his way again, axe in hand. Mrs. Flanagan was sweeping her front porch viciously when he opened her gate and approached. "Ma'am," he said politely, doffing his old hat, "Have you some chores I might do for you? Split some wood or kindling? Sharpen your knives; fix something?"

Katy Flanagan thought that he was asking for work for pay. "No," she said. "I got no extra money, taking in washing and ironing as I do." McGee tried to explain that he didn't want any pay, that he just wanted to do some good deeds for "widows 'n orphans."

Wow! That sure turned her hot tongue loose. "I'm no widow, and I'm no orphan and I make me own way. Nothing a low-down man can do that I can't". She accused McGee of trying to get on the best side of her so he could take her to bed but she'd have him know she was an honest woman who'd been cursed by a shiftless man, and you couldn't trust a one of the blaggards, and anyway her man would be back one of these days or years and she'd tell him what she thought of him, she would. On and on she went, getting madder by the minute, as McGee backed up to the gate, fearing that if he turned around he'd get clobbered by that broom. He could still hear her ranting when he was four doors up the street.

When he got to Mrs. Johnson's house he saw her coming out of her barn with a load of small wood in her arms. Hurrying to her, he took the wood into the kitchen woodbox, then went after another load. Helen Johnson was most appreciative. Her grandchildren were coming that weekend, she said, and she was baking up a storm. She offered him a cup of tea, explaining that she was out of coffee. McGee told her he was out of coffee too and then explained his mission. "I figure I'm going to die pretty soon, Miz Johnson," he said, "and I'm a-trying to do some good deeds so I won't be going to hellfire and damnation. You got some other things I could do for you, sharpen some knives or anything else?"

Mrs. Johnson was a nice lady. Yes, she had some knives that needed sharpening and a pair of scissors too and perhaps he could fix that hinge on the cellar door. As he worked on the tasks, they had some pleasant conversation. Leaving, McGee told her he'd drop in every so often to see if she needed some help. No, he wouldn't take any pay. He was just doing a good deed.

His next stop was at Aunt Lizzie's house. When he explained why he wanted to do good deeds, her eyes lit up. Yes, she could sure use a man around the house. She had a lot of things that ought to be done but would he start by chopping her some small wood and kindling. She had a lot of it in the shed. McGee noticed that there was a coffeepot on the range and thought of asking for a cup but thought it might be wise to wait until he'd done some work. After he had quite a pile, he went back to the kitchen and asked her if he'd done enough. And he smelled the coffee. No, Aunt Lizzie said, after she'd examined the pile he'd cut. Just a mite more.

After he'd split a lot more, he asked Aunt Lizzie if she had any more he could do, noticing that she was drinking a cup of the coffee and eating a cinnamon roll. She didn't offer any of either but asked him to bring down a mattress from the bedroom to air it out and then to haul out the rugs and beat them and the mattress with the carpet beater after he hung them on the clothesline. Now mattresses are mean critters to bring down narrow stairs. You just can't get a decent hold on them. They flop around and stick and jam but somehow McGee got them out in the yard, thinking that it would have been a lot easier if Aunt Lizzie had helped a bit. Beating those damned rugs wasn't any fun either. A dirty dusty job but he got it done.

It seemed that the instant he finished one job, Aunt Lizzie came up with another. She had a kerosene lamp in which the wick had fallen into the bowl. Could he snake it out and rethread it? There was a barrel in the cellar full of trash and rotten apples. Would Mr. McGee please haul it up and put it behind the shed? Would he please climb up on the roof to see if the chimney needed cleaning? Did the chicken coop need cleaning? McGee took a look at it and was sure that it did but he said no. He was getting very tired. Needed a cup of coffee or something. Finally when Aunt Lizzie proposed that he clean her attic, McGee rebelled. "I'll haul that damned mattress back up to your bedroom," he said, "but that's it." Again she didn't help him and wrestling the thing up those narrow stairs almost did him in. Exhausted, he sat down in a chair in the kitchen trying to catch his breath.

Eyeing the coffee pot on the range, it being past noon, McGee finally asked Aunt Lizzie if she might spare a cup. "No." she said. "There's only about one cup left in it and I always like to have a cup after my nap." She didn't even thank him for all his work.

On his way back to his cabin Old Man McGee was figuring out how many good deeds he'd done. "Let's see," he said aloud as he walked down the hill street. "At Miz Johnson's I hauled two loads of wood, sharpened three knives and those damned scissors and fixed the cellar door. That makes seven. And up at Aunt Lizzie's - hell, I can't even count how many. Make it thirteen and that makes twenty. Not a bad day's work, McGee. Hope old Saint Peter is a-counting."

But there was still another good deed to come. As he passed Mrs. Johnson's house, she came out to the gate holding a dollar bill. "Mr. McGee, would you do one more good deed for me? Will you take this up to Flynn's store and get two pound bags of coffee? I'm in the middle of baking and can't get away and I'm just dying for a cup of coffee. Have them grind it on the big red coffee grinder." McGee was sure tired but did the errand and enjoyed the aroma of the coffee beans being ground. When he returned with the two bags and eleven cents, Mrs. Johnson gave him one bag of coffee for himself and told him to keep the change.

Old Man McGee went home, brewed himself a fat cup of coffee, and went to bed, unafraid of the hereafter.

AUNT LIZZIE'S MULLED CIDER

The U.P. has always been known for its hard drinkers. So was Tioga. It wasn't just the cold winters and hard labor that made our men hit the bottle; it was mainly because the only place where they could gather together and have male companionship was Higley's Saloon. Few of them ever got really drunk (they didn't have the money) so they nursed their beers until closing time. Oh, there were one or two who might be considered real drunks, Billy Bones and Pete Ramos for instance, but for the most part our men just drank a little  and went home to bed. None of our women ever went to Higley's Saloon but they often sipped some of their chokecherry wine. A few bought Lydia Pinkham's Vegetable Compound, which was half alcohol, to taste when life got too tough for them. There were few teetotallers in Tioga.

Every year or two a wandering temperance preacher came to town to raise a little hell. Our people listened politely but when church was over they returned home for a little nip to pass the winter away. One of those preachers, however, the Reverend Zachariah Smith, once caused a lot of trouble in our town mainly because he enlisted Aunt Lizzie to help the cause. He was a good hellfire preacher but unlike the others who claimed we were committing all sorts of sins, the Reverend Zachariah had boiled them all down into one: the imbibing of alcohol.

Lord, how he raised Cain about drinking. It was EVIL, he shouted. "The Turks, Mohammedans, they prohibit any use of Al Kohol (He spelled it out) because their word for the Devil is Al Kohol. Don't tell me that them infidels have a better religion than us Christians, but at least they know that beer and whiskey and wine are the devil's work. It's the curse of our nation!"

From there he went on to tell what alcohol did to your system, and he showed two lantern slides to illustrate. The first showed a normal stomach nice and clean; the second, a decrepit organ riddled with red and green abnormalities. Sure was scary! "But it's your liver," he roared, "that takes the real beating. It shrivels when alcohol comes into it, and sooner or later you'll die and go to hell." He showed us a livid liver that no one would want to have. I was so scared I resolved that I would never take a nip of anything alcoholic again. I remembered that my beloved Grampa Gage often took a slug from the black bottle he carried in his hip pocket and so I worried about him. And I myself had sneaked a little snort from the bottle of brandy and also from the bottle of Scotch whiskey my father kept in the cellar way. They tasted terrible, especially the Scotch, more like medicine than castor oil did. No, I'd never take another taste of The Devil so long as I lived.

Alas, I must confess I broke that resolution and gradually worked my way through beer and wine and bourbon to Scotch whiskey. In my college years, those when Prohibition ruled the land, I drank bathtub gin and moonshine on occasion, and once after Homecoming at the University of Iowa a policeman intercepted me as I was walking down an empty street with a flashlight. I told him I was Diogenes, looking for an honest man. "Well, you've found him," he said, "Come with me; Diogenes." It was the only night I ever spent in jail. So I made that early resolution all over again and promptly broke it. In my old age, I find that two fingers of whiskey at Happy Hour gives me a nice feeling of mellowness and serenity while one finger (or perhaps a thumb) helps me to have sweet dreams. But I never get drunken and I feel sorry for those who compulsively use the lovely poison to escape their troubles. Nor do I take my whiskey straight. "A little bit of water makes the whiskey go down, the whiskey go down, the whiskey go down. Oh, a little bit of water helps the whiskey go down, in a most delightful way." It helps me forget my aching old bones and makes me feel young again.

But back to my story. After painting our liquor-riddled organs scarlet and black, the Reverend Zachariah ranted about what liquor did to the families of boozers. "Al Kohol, the devil, wrecks families," he shouted. "Women and children starve when the wage earner wastes his pay on liquor." He lost us there. None of our women or children starved because of the money spent on a few beers at Higley's saloon. They always had potatoes in the cellar and illegal venison or fish in the shed. Sensing our negative response, the preacher became evangelical. "In this congregation," he insisted, "there are one or more persons who can be my hands, who can carry out my mission to rid this village of the curse of Al Kohol. Just one person can make all the difference. If any one of you feel that you can carry the torch of temperance, please see me after the service."

The only one who did was Aunt Lizzie. She told the Reverend Zachariah how impressed she was with his presentation and that she knew firsthand of the evils of drink because all of her husbands had imbibed and died. As a poor widow she would be glad to carry the torch of temperance and be his hands, but she didn't know how to begin. The Reverend Zachariah sold her two hundred copies of a tract on the evils of Al Kohol for ten dollars and told her to make a survey of the homes in Tioga and to leave a copy in each of them, and to try to persuade the saloon keeper to mend his ways. He also gave her free fifty copies of a card that read "Lips that touch liquor shall never touch mine" to distribute to the young girls of Tioga. They were to sign it, he said, as a perpetual pledge.

For his purposes, the Reverend Zachariah couldn't have picked a better person. Aunt Lizzie was our town gossip. Each day she walked our hill street from home to home collecting and spreading the rumors and tidbits of the day, especially those that could cause trouble. Some called her The Raven, the huge black bird that flies over the land searching for carrion. She was the nosiest person in town. Completely insensitive to criticism or rejection, and very tenacious, she roamed Tioga leaving a lot of hurt feelings in her wake. I suppose she served a useful purpose as our town's newspaper, helping us to know what had happened to each other. When the Catholic Church bell failed one morning to ring Angeles, Aunt Lizzie soon found out why. Old Francoise Pitu had been having an argument with the priest and besides his arthritis was acting up again. Lempi Salo had been kicked in the head by the cow she was milking. Dr. Gage had to put in five stitches. Pete Ramos was in jail again up at the town hall. Charlie Olafson had found him passed out in Mrs. Carlson's petunias. One of the high-school girls had told her that the new English teacher didn't wear any panties under her skirts. Pete Hemel's horse got in a clover patch and foundered. All bloated up and like to die. "They say that the priest is about to discharge his old ugly housekeeper and get a pretty younger one." So it went day after day as Aunt Lizzie made her rounds.

But now she had a cause and a calling. The Reverend Zachariah had asked her to be his hands, and the Lord's hands, in the battle against Al Kohol, the Devil. She had to take a survey to identify all those who had fallen from grace by way of the bottle. She had 200 temperance tracts to hand out and pledge cards to give to the girls. Aunt Lizzie was in full glory. She couldn't wait to get started.

Having memorized some selections from the temperance booklet, and never being at a loss for words anyway, Aunt Lizzie sure gave Tioga a good working over. Oh there were doors slammed in her face when the news of her crusade preceded her but she just tucked a copy of the tract under the door, jotted down the name of the householder in her notebook as a probable sinner and went on to the next home. When she was able to get inside, she gave her spiel, tried to get them to pay ten cents for the tract to recoup her investment, and if they refused she left it with them free. Many just told her to her face that it was none of her business if any one in the family drank. Didn't faze Aunt Lizzie in the least. She just preached a little harder, loving every moment of it. Altogether she became the worst nuisance our town had known since 1915, the Year of the Mouse, when hordes of them invaded our village. So far as we could tell, Aunt Lizzie converted few if any of us to the cause of temperance. Probably we just imbibed a bit more.

God-fearing, but fearing nothing else, one evening she even had the guts to enter Higley's Saloon where no woman or child had ever set foot to leave a handful of her temperance tracts. Higley leaped over the bar, picked her up in his arms, took her outside and sat her down carefully in a snowbank. "You try that one more time and I'll throw you over the fence," he roared fiercely. Aunt Lizzie didn't try it again but it gave her the nice feeling of being a Christian martyr. Altogether she was having a ball.

For some reason, she had not visited our home until one bitterly cold winter afternoon. Perhaps she remembered how our cat, Puuko, had clawed her when she insisted on sitting in his chair, or perhaps it was because she knew my father was openly hostile to her. He'd told her outright that she was a nasty old busybody always stirring up trouble and that she was unwelcome in his house. It was a good thing that he was out making calls on his patients when she came to the door.

"May I come in, Mrs. Gage?" Aunt Lizzie said to my mother. "I'm about friz to death and fancy I'd better warm up before I go the rest of the way home." Of course mother had her come in and sat her in the chair next to our big baseburner, the hard coal stove. Aunt Lizzie was sure shivering, really shaking. "I've been preaching the temperance gospel over in Finn Town back of the mine and only one of them, Mrs. Rautila, the Holy Jumper, invited me inside. That wind, Mrs. Gage, is terrible today but the Lord's work must be done." Her shivering had begun to subside.

I knew mother was worrying that Dad might come home any minute and wanted her out of there before he did but, always the lady, she had to find ways of being hospitable. "I have some sweet cider heating on the kitchen stove," she said. "My husband always likes a mug of hot mulled cider when he comes home on such a cold day. Would you like some, Mrs. Campton? It will really warm you."

Aunt Lizzie was suspicious. "What's mulled cider?" she asked. "If it's the same as hard cider, thank you, no!"

"Oh no, it's sweet cider. We heat it first, then Cully gets a poker white hot in the dining room wood stove and puts it into the cider mug where it hisses. Mulling cider gives it a special flavor. Do try some." Mother motioned to me to get the Toby mugs and put the poker in the stove. Just then my father entered the back door off the kitchen. He was frozen too. "Good!" he said when he saw the cider heating on the kitchen stove. "I've been thinking of hot mulled cider all the way home. Oh, it's cold out there!"

Mother hurriedly explained about Aunt Lizzie and begged him to be pleasant. "I couldn't turn that poor old woman away, John," she insisted. "After she's warmed up and had a mug of hot cider I'll find some way to get rid of her." Dad growled but gave in. "Cully," he said, "You be sure to put the usual three fingers of brandy in my mug after you put the poker in it." Then he stalked into the living room, gave Aunt Lizzie a curt nod and started to read his Chicago Tribune.

I got the brandy from the cellar way, put the poker in the woodstove and turned up the draft lever on the stovepipe to get a hot fire, then fetched four Toby mugs (those with the funny faces baked into the clay) and put them side by side by the stove. Mother and Aunt Lizzie were chatting in the living room and being studiously ignored by my father. I'd planned to bring the hot cider from the kitchen stove to fill the mugs but the handle was too hot so I brought back the mugs to the kitchen putting Dad's brandy in one of them. After it was filled and ready for the white hot poker, I brought them back to the dining room stove and had fun with the mulling.

Proudly I bore the first two mugs, one for Aunt Lizzie and the other to my father, then went back to mull some for Mother and me. In just a few moments my father stomped past me into the kitchen to get more brandy. He was angry. "I told you to put three fingers of brandy in the cider, not one," he said to me as he passed. "Might as well be drinking hot swamp water." I couldn't argue with him because I was busy with the steaming poker but I really had put brandy in the mug. Yes, I had!

Then the thought came to me that somehow I'd mixed up the mugs and had given his to Aunt Lizzie. Oh, oh! I brought mother her cider and sat where I could watch the effects, if any. They were soon forthcoming. "My, my!" Aunt Lizzie exclaimed, "That's the best cider I ever drank in my life. It sure warms my innards!" Soon she was so warm she had to move her chair further from the stove and a bit later she began to giggle. No one in Tioga had ever heard Aunt Lizzie giggle. Mother couldn't believe her ears but kept a patter of conversation going only to find that whatever she said was greeted by that giggle. Yes, I must have given her the mug with the brandy in it. Her speech began to get a bit slurred by the time her mug was emptied and when she suggested she might like a bit more of that mulled cider if there were any left, my father, who had also made his own diagnosis, spoke for the first time, "No," he said firmly. "It's all gone and I'll have Cully hitch up the horse to the sleigh and take you home."

When I returned for Aunt Lizzie she had a helluva time putting on her coat even with mother's help and I had to support her as she staggered to the cutter. Getting her out of it when I reached her house was even more difficult but finally I got her through the door and into a chair.

I fully expected to catch bloody hell when I entered our back door where mother was waiting for me. "Is she all right?" mother asked anxiously. I reassured her. "Now, Cully, remember this: you are not to tell a living soul about what happened," she commanded.

"But I already have," I responded. "Aunt Lizzie begged me to tell her what was wrong with her so I did. I told her she was drunk." Mother moaned.

"Suddenly my father was there in the kitchen with us. "All I want to know is if you did it on purpose?" he asked sternly.

"No," I replied. "I just got those two mugs mixed up. I don't know how it happened. Honest!"

Dad grinned his crooked grin. "Here," he said, giving me a new silver quarter. "If you'd done it on purpose, it would have been a half dollar instead. That old buzzard will think twice before she stops in here again."

I don't know just what impact the experience had on Aunt Lizzie. I do know that her crusade sort of seemed to peter out and peace again returned to Tioga.

THE HONEY TREE

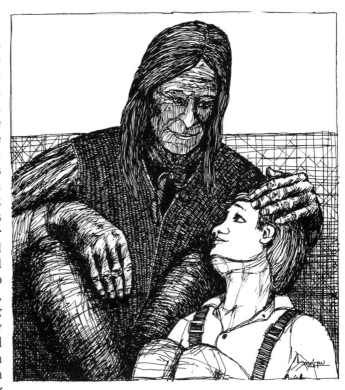

Pete Half Shoes, our resident full-blooded Ojibway Indian, was one of my favorite people in Tioga, and with the other boys I often visited him and Mabel, his pet skunk, to while away a few hours before supper time. Pete liked kids, and dogs and kids always know when a man does or doesn't. Not that he ever really showed his feelings. His copper brown face seemed carved in red granite and we often did our utmost to get him to laugh or smile, making silly faces, doing silly things, saying nutty stuff, but he never batted an eye. Just sat there on the porch of his cabin smoking his pipe, petting Mabel, and watching our antics with complete impassivity.

Pete Half Shoes didn't talk much either. If you asked him a question, he'd consider it for a long time before answering, and when he did reply it was usually a single word or phrase. But he would willingly walk quite a ways in the woods to identify a strange animal track we had discovered. "Marten," he said, "Pine marten." A wonderful carver, he could whittle out a tiny canoe, or a frog, or squirrel in only a few minutes. Most of the kids who lived uptown in Tioga had something Pete Half Shoes had carved for them. Being with him in the woods was a revelation and an education. He taught us what was good to eat and what was not. He showed us to see with strange eyes, noticing things like the trail of a pine snake on the forest floor or the very high-pitched song of the grasshopper sparrow. "Indian bandage," he would say, pointing to the leaf of a hairy plantain. "Put on cut; no more bleed."

Unfortunately, most of the people in our town didn't appreciate old Pete Half Shoes the way we kids did. He didn't have a job nor want one, spending most of his time wandering in the woods, fishing and hunting, or every evening just before the St. Paul train pulled in he'd be in the corner of his favorite booth at Higley's Saloon drinking. It was always beer and rarely more than three bottles and he nursed them carefully so he wouldn't have to go home before ten o'clock. Only once had he ever got really drunk and that was when he tried to enlist in the army at the beginning of World War I and was told he was too old. That was a beauty, a ten day drunk, but he recovered and went the rhythm of his days thereafter.

But I think it was because of Mabel that most of our people didn't approve of Pete Half Shoes. He'd found the baby skunk and descented it when it was just a baby, made a pet of it, and often carried Mabel on his shoulder even when he went to Flynn's store to buy groceries. I liked Mabel. She was fun to play with; she liked being stroked; she liked kids to pick her up. People said that she was old Pete's bed partner but what was wrong with that? I've slept with a lot of cats in my day though my mother never knew it. When they howled outside my back bedroom window on a cold or rainy night I just had to let them in. People said that Pete Half Shoes probably lived in filth because of that skunk but that wasn't true.

Once, when I hadn't seen him around for several days and the door was open I went in timorously to find him sitting in a chair reading. "Are you all right, Pete?" I asked. "I've been worrying about you." "Old Pete, OK," he replied, gave me a bit of maple sugar, then sat with me on his porch for a long time. I put my head against his leg, as a spaniel does to his master's knee and said, "I, I like you, Pete." After a moment he put his old hand on my head and said, "You good boy, Cully," And incredibly, he smiled. I felt anointed. Old Pete Half Shoes had smiled.

Shortly after this had happened I overheard a conversation, or rather an argument between my mother and father. "John," she said to him. "I want you to forbid Cully's going up to Pete Half Shoes' place so often. I don't think it's good for him to be around that shiftless drunken old Indian so much."

"No, damned if I will," replied my father, "and you mustn't either. Pete's no shiftless Indian and though he's a regular down at Higley's Saloon every evening, he never gets drunk. I respect Pete Half Shoes. He was an Indian Scout in the regular army for many years, took part in the campaign against Geronimo and the Apaches, fought with Roosevelt in the Spanish American War, and gets a good enough pension so he doesn't have to work."

"But that skunk? And he never goes to the sauna?" Mother interjected. "You don't either, Edyth," said my father. "He's a clean man and a proud man. You know how he marches with the other few veterans in our Fourth of July parades and he puts up an American flag in his window every morning and takes it down every night. He pays his bills at Flynn's store and never causes any trouble. I'm glad to have Cully have a chance to be with him. He may learn more from old Pete than he does in school."

So I had no trouble being with the old Indian any time I wanted to. I helped him pick berries and was fascinated to see how he dried them, sometimes in a pan on the stove, sometimes on his roof, blueberries, raspberries, thimble-berries and even cranberries. Pete never canned them as our people always did. He didn't have a garden either. When I asked him why not, he just grunted, "Squaw work. Pete got no squaw." He bought his winter potatoes from his neighbors or traded them for the venison he'd shot in season or out. Every spring he made a batch of maple syrup and boiled it down to maple sugar and I helped him gather wood for the boiling down.

He had another source of sweetening too as I found out one summer's day. One hot afternoon in July Fisheye, Mullu and I were planning to take a swim in Lake Tioga. As we took the shortcut through the grove to go down Company Field hill, we saw Pete Half Shoes putting a pork and bean can in the clover. Curious of course, we had to go over to see what he was doing. "Old Pete hunting for honey tree," he said after a long silence. "Sugar for winter." Suddenly he plopped the can down, then slipped a bit of birch bark under its opening. We could hear the bee buzzing inside. Then, standing upright, he let the bee go, watching where it went, and placing some poplar shoots to line its path toward the grove. You couldn't see that honey bee very long, so Pete had to catch several before he was sure of the line. Of course we begged to catch some honeybees too, and he let us but when Mullu caught a big bumblebee in the can, Pete said, "No. Bumblebee no good for honey. Get little one like so." He had me go to the fence line of the grove and waved me to the right or left as he let the bees go until he had the direction right. Then he moved over to one side about fifty feet and started getting bee lines again with other bees. Tiring of it, we kids headed for the lake.

One bitter morning the next winter I swiped some new cookies from the jar in the pantry and with Mullu brought them up to Pete Half Shoes. He thanked me and asked if we wanted to go with him to cut down a honey tree to get some honey. We were overjoyed, of course. Pete had located it by triangulation the summer before and when we put our ears to the trunk of the basswood tree we could hear humming inside.

"But won't the bees sting us?" Fisheye asked. Pete thought a long time, then said "No!" I'd carried his one man cross-cut saw and Mullu had Pete's ax and Pete had two water pails. Soon they were put to use. First Pete chopped the kerf so the tree would fall on its back opposite the little slit through which the bees had entered and left. A few bees zoomed out but when they hit the cold air, it just zapped them and they fell dead in the snow below. Then Mullu and I took turns sawing and finally the big tree fell with more bees getting zapped. We never got stung once though we sure expected it. Then Pete made two half cuts above and below the entrance hole or slit, let more bees swarm out to die, and then with the axe cut out a slab to reveal the honeycomb inside.

Lord there was a lot of honey in that basswood tree. Taking off his mittens Pete just scooped the stuff into the pails, honeycomb, larvae, bees and all. Didn't look too appetizing but Pete dug out a handful of honey and frozen bees from the trunk to stuff it in his mouth. "Bees best of all," he said. So, of course we had to try it too. Incredibly sweet it was, and very sticky. I couldn't help but spit out some of the honey-coated grubs or whatever they were and soon I'd had enough honey. But Pete Half Shoes insisted we each take a big chunk of it home with us, something we eventually regretted for our mittens never lost their stickiness till April.

Then suddenly Mullu who had been chomping on his hunk of bee mess gave a howl, a scream, and ran around in circles, alternately holding his mouth and sticking his tongue out as far as he could. Must have got a live bee. And then, for the first time we heard the old Indian laugh. Oh how he cackled! A rusty sort of cackle and laugh. With his tongue hanging out, Mullu said he had to get home so I went with him, carrying the axe and saw, and letting Pete to carry the pails of honey back later.

When we reached the grove, I asked Mullu if it still hurt awfully badly. "Naw," he said. "I didn't get stung at all. I just wanted to make old Pete Half Shoes laugh. And I did!"

But I had made him smile.

SLIMBER TELLS THE TRUTH

It all happened because Sally Griggs, our third grade teacher, invited her father and sister from Chicago to see the town where she had taught the year before and would again this year. They'd arrive on the morning train and leave on the evening one. Sally's letters about Tioga and its people and the forest had intrigued them greatly and they hoped to see as much as they could in the short time at their disposal. Now really there's not much to see in Tioga so Sally arranged with old man Marchand who owned the livery stable to

provide her with a horse and a two seated buckboard so they could drive up along the Tioga River to the Haysheds where the stream broke through a big chain of granite hills in a spectacular waterfall and rapids. "Oh yes," she told Marchand, "and please find me a good driver, one who knows the land and its history and who's a good storyteller. I'll pack lunch for the lot of us. Leave at ten and be back here about four in the afternoon."

Marchand knew just the man to be the driver, he said, Slimber Jim Vester. Knew horses and the country and sure could tell stories. Sally vaguely recalled the name. "Is he the one they tell about who caught a trout with a posthole digger, the one who crossed a blue heron with a duck? The one they call the biggest liar in Tioga?" "Oui, ma femme, Slimber he the man," answered Marchand. "He tell you stories for sure, oui!"

Slimber was glad to see that Marchand not only gave him the new buckboard with two seats and cushions but also Celeste, the big brown horse, to pull it. He'd been afraid he'd get old Maude, notoriously the slowest horse in town, whose back legs were said to walk backward when the front ones went forward. Celeste clopped along smartly and soon Slimber was at the door of the boarding house. Jumping down and doffing his cap politely to reveal that saintly face of his framed in white whiskers, he introduced himself and Celeste. Sally greeted him warmly and presented her sister, June, and her father Mr. William Griggs. A lawyer from Chicago, she said, who also wrote articles about the many places he traveled. "So don't tell us any of your little fibs," she added.

Slimber felt insulted. "I don't tell fibs," he said. "I tell only big fancy lies and them only to those bums down at the saloon. I'll tell you only the truth, the whole truth, and nothing but the truth, so help me."

"God!" said the lawyer from Chicago.

As Slimber was handing up the girls to the rear seats and the father to his, Sally asked him to drive first past the old mine and then down the back road to Lake Tioga before they went up the road alongside the river. "My father and sister just must see that lovely lake," she said. "There are fifteen pine-covered islands in it and..."

"Begging your pardon, Ma'am," interrupted Slimber. "There's only fourteen of 'em and Flat Island doesn't have a tree on it since it burnt off six, no seven years ago." A stickler for the truth was Slimber Vester.

Of course they had to stop at the mine to see the cave-in, and Slimber filled them in with some of its history. "At one time this was the deepest iron mine in the world," he said proudly. "One of its shafts went down a mile. Even when it was twenty below zero on the surface it was so warm down there the men only worked short shifts, ten hours a day rather than the usual twelve. Hard to believe now," he said waving around at the abandoned buildings and desolate rock piles, " but when I was a young man we had a thousand men working here."

"Were you a miner?" asked June.

"Well, yes and no," said the old man. "I worked on surface, carpenter work and such. Never wanted to go underground though the pay was better. Saw too many men come up with their heads cracked open like hazelnuts and their brains leaking down over their ears. Rocks fall from ceiling of the stopes - them's the big rooms where they've taken out the ore. This here cave-in come because the Mining Company robbed too much ore off the pillars that supported the ceiling." Slimber for a moment almost started telling the story of how August Keski, riding the skip down with two cases of dynamite, saved himself when the hoisting cable broke by jumping up in the air just before the cage hit bottom but he resisted the temptation. Too bad! It was a good story the way he could tell it but no sir, he wasn't going to tell a single lie all day. No sir!

Instead he told them about the blue snow they had when the mine was working. That raised some eyebrows until he explained that this was a hard ore mine, with specular hematite, silvery blue in color, not red like the ordinary hematite in most mines. "When the big crusher was working hard, grinding up the chunks of ore that came up from the bowels of the earth, the dust covered everything including the snow with a light blue color." Noting that they were doubting, Slimber found a little piece of specular hematite to show them. As its fine scales glistened in the sun it looked more silver than blue. "Just the same, snow looks blue when crusher working," insisted Slimber.

To change the subject Slimber pointed out the tall stone smoke stack that still stood above the stone walls of the engine room building. "Every night about sundown thousands of swallows circle around that stack and ever so often one of them folds its wings and drops down into the chimney like a rock. Don't know how they stop or find their nest but every morning they come out at sunrise again. Worth seeing. Ever see that, Miss Sally?" he asked. She said no, but that she'd sure be looking now.

Back on the buckboard it was pleasant being out of the sun and under the tall trees that arched over the sandy ruts of the road. Very quiet and very peaceful with only the sounds of Celeste's hooves breaking the silence. At one of the turns a little road branched off to the left. "That's the old stagecoach road," Slimber said. "Tioga in the old, old days, was just a stagecoach stop where they changed horses and drivers, just barns and a sleeping shack or two. The road really was a military road, running from Green Bay in Wisconsin up to Fort Wilkins on the Keewenaw peninsula where they kept a garrison of soldiers, I dunno why, mebbe to fight the Indians. Anyway, once a week in the summer a stage coach was hauled along this old military road, bringing up mail, some supplies, and the payroll for the soldiers. No railroads back then."

"They say that once some highway bandits tried to shanghai that there payroll but the drivers whipped up their horses and the paymaster inside the coach threw out the money bags in a narrow part of the road where them men a-chasing them couldn't pass. I dunno if the story is true. I hunted all along that old road when I was a boy and never found any gold pieces. That's what they paid them with in the old days."

Out of the corner of his eye, Slimber noticed that Mr. Griggs had been writing in his notebook, things like: "Mine, one mile deep"? "Blue snow"? "Thousand swallows drop in chimney like rocks?" and now "Stagecoach money sacks."? Slimber didn't like those question marks one bit. Hell, he'd been telling the truth all the time.

When they got to the shores of Lake Tioga, Slimber stopped the horse, and the four people went down to the sandy beach to get a better look at it. A beautiful lake, a large one, seven miles long and a mile wide, Slimber told them. It seemed brim full, with the waters lapping the base of the labrador tea bushes at its edge. It had rocky points too and the first of the pine-crowned islands were clearly visible. The water was so clear every pebble could be seen. High hills, mostly granite, surrounded the lake as far as one could see.

"How's the fishing?" asked Mr. Griggs.

Slimber paused a bit before answering, remembering what a bad time he'd had when he caught Old Lunker, that great northern pike, and the bear stole it from him just before he reached town. He was tempted to tell the tale because, after all it was God's truth, but if his own townspeople never believed him, these foreigners from Down Below wouldn't either. So all he said was that there were bass, walleye and the biggest Northern pike you could find in any lake in the U.P. His arms ached to show them how big Old Lunker really was, but he resisted.

He did tell them that once in the old days there had been a steamboat on the lake. That raised their eyebrows. Why would you need a steamboat on a lake that was only seven miles long and a mile wide? "Well," said Slimber defensively, "It was really only a tugboat they'd hauled up on the plank road from Marquette, but it had a real steam engine that burned wood. They used it to haul rafts of hardwood from the hills across the lake to fuel the big boilers at the mine before the railroad came to town." Slimber could see Mr. Griggs writing "Steamboat????" (But it was true. I, Cully, played on the tug's wreckage when I was a boy and still remember the rusty smokestack that emerged from the lake at the place it had been beached.)

As they drove along the south side of Lake Tioga to its end, Slimber pointed out some depressions in the ground. "Those are the deer pits," he said. "In the old days, the first settlers and Indians used to dig deep pits in the deer trails that deer then used to migrate when the deep snows came. Then they planted deeply in them some very sharp stakes before covering the pits with a light layer of branches. The deer would fall into these pits and skewer themselves. Bullets cost too much those days." Slimber said. "Men had to eat. No, they don't migrate like they used to. Now they yard up in a cedar swamp to make it through the winter." Mr. Griggs made an entry in his notebook. Slimber couldn't see if it had the usual question mark.

"How did they know where to put the deer pits?" Mr. Griggs asked. It was a challenge. "There's miles and miles of forest here."

"That's easy explained," replied Slimber, slapping the reins on Celeste's rump. "Deer form runways, travel the same path often enough so you can see it. They usually travel single file. Down here as they had to go around the lake on their migration south they'd trod down the path for centuries. Hard to see now 'cause they don't do it any more but when I was a boy that migrating path was about a foot deep still. So the old-timers just put their staked pits in the deep ruts." Mr. Griggs erased something in his notebook.

Soon they were trotting along the road that ran beside the Tioga River. Sally saw a big bird flying overhead. "What a big crow!" she exclaimed, pointing. "Naw, that's no crow. That's a raven" said Slimber. "Hear him a-croakin'? Ravens don't caw like crows. They croak. They got a bell sound too that they make. Not many people ever hear that bell sound. Ravens don't fly south; they stay up here with us all winter."

"Quoth the raven 'Nevermore'," said June.

"Naw, ravens can't talk," said Slimber, "but crows can." He told them the story about Nikki Sippola's pet crow that almost broke up their marriage by saying, "I come back." It was a true story but Slimber knew none of the three would believe a word of it."

The Tioga is a beautiful river running thirty-forty feet wide through the forest but in summertime it is usually only about three or four feet deep at most. Many rocks lift their heads above the current. Slimber had been regaling his passengers with stories of the old logging days and the river drives of the spring when thousands of huge logs were floated down the river to Lake Tioga.

"It's hard for me to believe that the kind of logs you describe could ever be floated down such a shallow stream," "Mr. Griggs said. "I think you told us some of them were five or six feet across at the butt. A big log like that would weigh a ton. Surely, sir, you have been exaggerating a little. Weren't those logs really smaller, say about two feet across?"

That irritated Slimber. "Just look at those old stumps alongside the road," he said. "They're five to seven feet across. These were cork pine, Mister, virgin pine, sometimes one hundred fifty to two hundred feet tall. You saw one down and when it crash it sounds like thunder."

"I still don't see how they could be floated down this stream," Mr. Griggs objected.

"Ah hell, Mister," Slimber said. "This is summer low water. In spring flood the Tioga is six, eight feet deeper. And then they had logging dams upstream, holding back lakes of water that they released through the sluice gates to send a wall of water down that could float any log any size." Then Slimber told them of the log jams and how the rivermen with their pikes and peavies would have to tease out the key log, or sometimes dynamite it, to get the river of logs flowing again. He told them how the men would ride the logs, birling, rolling them with their caulked boots to steer them a mite when they had to. He told them about some of the tragic deaths and miraculous rescues that had occurred. Completely fascinated by his stories, the passengers often also showed little signs of scepticism.

Mr. Griggs pulled out a big gold watch from his vestpocket and opened the lid. "Oh, half past noon already," he said. "I'm hungry. Is there somewhere near here where we can have our picnic lunch? I know the girls must have something good in that hamper you put behind the seats."

"Yeah, there's a fine place just around the next bend," Slimber replied. "A fine spring there and a little clearing right above the river."

It was indeed a lovely spot. Taking off Celeste's bridle, he gave her a half pail of oats and some hay from the buckboard, then showed the Griggs around. "There's the big spring," Slimber pointed, "and there's the little one. Best water south of Lake Superior." The girls opened the hamper, spread out a tablecloth with four cups and plates. "Oh, I brung my own grub," said Slimber, pulling out of the pocket of his coat in the buckboard a big onion, a chunk of bologna and some korpua, but they insisted he share their food. The bottle of milk, however, was warm, so as it cooled in the lower spring, Slimber made them a birch bark cup, peeling a piece of bark from a nearby tree, rolling it into a cone, folding the lower half up to the brim and then fastening that with a cleft stick. All of them had to try it and agreed that they'd never had such ice-cold delicious water.

"You kin boil water in a birch bark basket," Slimber said. "I've made lots of coffee and tea that way in my day." Mr. Griggs made a mental note: Boil water in birch bark???????"

The girls had been prowling around the edges of the clearing and brought back some berries. Slimber took one look and plucked out three big blue ones. "Good thing you didn't try to eat these," he said. "Them's aconite - bad poison. Four of 'em would put you in a casket. The other's are all right: blueberries, thimbleberries, one red raspberry, and some wintergreen berries." He ate one of each in the interest of eternal truth and was glad to see that for once they believed him because they tasted them.

Their doubts began again, however, when he found a Venus fly trap, the pitcher plant, and told them it ate flies. It was old and dried up and so didn't have any of the flies and bugs it usually contains. Then he found a lady-slipper, also long out of bloom and a bit bedraggled. "Educated fella told me once this lady slipper, they also call it an Indian moccasin, is the only North American orchid," he said, "but I don't know what's an orchid." They explained but said it didn't look like any orchid they'd ever viewed.

Packing up their stuff after the meal and with a last drink of spring water from the birch bark cup, they resumed their journey and soon were at the Haysheds. Tying Celeste to a tree, Slimber led them first by way of the upper trail to where the river had broken through the huge granite hills and where in the old days a logging dam had been constructed. (It has always been one of my favorite spots in the U.P.) Above the remnants of the old dam there's a great marsh where you can see for miles. "Yeah, they could store plenty of water there for floating the logs," Slimber said. "it was a lake a third as big as Tioga." He led the way to where they could peer over the granite cliff to see the water plunging fifty feet in a series of cascades around a huge waterworn granite hillock in the middle. Not much of the old dam remained but Slimber showed them where the sluice gate had been located and the log apron and flume were. "You ought to see it in the spring flood," said Slimber. "Then it's just one big waterfall."

The Griggs were impressed. "This is one of the most beautiful spots I've ever seen," said Sally.

"Let's take the lower trail," said Slimber. "It'll give you a better view," but as they did so, they found a dead porcupine in the path. Slimber looked it over carefully. "I'd say it was killed either by a bobcat or lynx. See, the bottom's all eaten out. Them wildcats are the only thing will kill a porcupine. They flip them over and chew out their insides." As they made their way to the bottom of the falls and oohed and ohed about them, Slimber showed them some of the quills he'd plucked off the porky, pointing out the sharp barbs on their ends.

"Why they look like a crochet needle," June said, "only much sharper."

"Sure are sharp," Slimber agreed. "Hard to pull out even with pliers. And if they break off, they work their way all through the flesh. A Finn man over by Halfway got one in his foot and it traveled all the way up to his knee before it come out. And I know of a dog that had a quill go to his heart and kill him." Slimber could just see Mr. Griggs putting down more question marks in that damned notebook of his but he gave each of them a big quill to take home for a souvenir.

Slimber was kind of quiet on the way home. They had to have another drink from the birch bark cup at the spring and June asked if she could keep it. Then Mr. Griggs asked Slimber about what fish were in the river.

"Mainly brook trout," Slimber replied. "Range from six to twelve inches mainly. Good eating though, any size. Also there's chubs and shiners and hornadays and a few big suckers."

"How do you fish for trout?" asked Mr. Griggs. Maybe he couldn't stand the silence.

"Oh usually with a goverment pole - that's an alder branch, a fishline and hook and worm. Not hard to catch. Once in a while we just tickle them." Slimber knew immediately that he should have had more sense than say that even if it were true.

"Tickle trout?" Mr. Griggs' voice was incredulous. Slimber explained how it was done but the more he talked the more they doubted him. Dammit, he'd have to show them. If he could! Trout were scarier this time of season. Tickling was better in the spring. But when they got to a plank culvert where a little stream crossed the road, Slimber saw a likely place, a little pool just below a new beaver dam, not far from the river. "Well, let me give her a try here," he said. "I don't guarantee it but I might just be able to show you how it's done anyway." He took off his shirt and lowered his arm very carefully into the pool and waited some time as the Griggs people watched. Then suddenly the arm came up with a big fish that he flung on the bank. "Ah hell!" exclaimed Slimber. "Just a big red horse sucker but that's how we tickle trout, Mister. Let yer hand lie there quiet till a fish swims over it, then slowly stroke it till you feel the gills, then heave 'em out on the bank."

"Well, I'll be damned!" said Mr. Griggs.

They stopped only one other time on the way home to give the horse a drink at a little pond that lapped the side of the road. Beside it was a big birch tree that had been girdled deeply by a beaver. Although Slimber told them that beavers have two three-inch long curved brown teeth sharp as a razor, they found it hard to believe they could have gnawed such large chips from such a big tree. While they waited, Slimber picked some chokecherries from a near-by bush and gave them a few for tasting. Then as they winced from the puckering of their lips he said that chokecherries made the best wine in the U.P. They doubted that too. An overturned pine stump showed signs, Slimber said, that it had been done by a bear eating ants. "Them ants, they're the bear's salt and pepper," said Slimber and out came Mr. Grigg's notebook again.

Only one other occurrence happened on the way back. Suddenly, Celeste snorted, then balked, then tore down the road as fast as she could while the girls screamed and clung to their seats. "Bear smell!" said Slimber holding tight to the reins. "I smelled it. Didn't you folks?" They hadn't.

Driving home in a horse and buggy always seems to take a lot longer than going some place. Finally, to break the silence Mr. Griggs asked Slimber if he hunted as well as fished.

"Why sure," said Slimber, suprised at the question. "Everybody hunts up here in the U.P., in season and out. Except for bacon and salt pork not many of our families ever buy store meat. Oh, some raise and butcher a steer or have a few pigs, but it's the game as feeds us through the winter till the fish come. I get me a deer or two each year and lots of rabbits, ducks, and partridge. I like partridge hunting best."

"How do you hunt partridge?" Mr. Griggs was passing time.

"Well, some shoot them on the wing but they use too many shells. Me, I like to spot them on the ground and shoot 'em before they cackle and fly off. Walk slow and shoot fast. Sometimes they'll fly up in a tree and then it's easy pickings."

"I thought you used a pointer dog to locate them," Mr. Griggs interjected.

"Naw, not me. Oh the Dudes from Down Below do bring up some of them fancy dogs to point pat and then retrieve, but as for me if I had a dog I'd want a barker. Had one long ago, and he sure was good. Soon as he'd see a partridge he start yapping like crazy and the pat would fly up into the nearest tree every time and I'd shoot him easy. Only had him one season. He got chewed up all to hell by another dog and died. Then I used an alarm clock for a season or two....."

"An alarm clock?" Mr. Griggs was fumbling for his notebook.

"Yah," said Slimber. "That works too, just like the barking. You wind it up and then when you think you see a pat, you turn it on ringing, and the bird goes up in the nearest tree." Slimber was about to tell of his old horse Joshua who used to point partridge with his left front leg but, seeing the skeptical expression on the lawyer's face, he skipped it. Too bad. Joshua did point partridge.

At last they had left the hills and were back on the long plains bordering the river. They were beautiful with white daisies, orange Indian paint brush, some early goldenrod and a few splotches of pink fireweed. And, of course, blueberry bushes.

"Slimber, why aren't there any trees here on the plain?" asked Sally. "Did they use to farm this land?"

"No Maam," the old man replied. "This land been burned over so many times, couldn't even grow hay. Pete Ramos' pappy, he used to burn it over every other year to make bigger blueberries. Sure did, too. Something about ashes that makes fine blueberries. We used to fill pailfuls here but one year old man Ramos he let his fire get away from him and we sure had a godawful forest fire and they put him jail for setting it. Still some good blueberries here but not like it was."

"You mean that someone would set a forest fire just to get blueberries?" Mr. Griggs asked. Slim didn't even answer, just slapped Celeste's butt with the reins to get her a-moving.

Finally, when they got back to Sally's boarding house, the two girls thanked Slimber profusely for his "entertaining stories" and the porcupine quills and the birch bark cup but Mr. Griggs said he'd ride down to the livery stable with him to pay "the fees".

"Entertaining stories," they'd said, thought Slimber. Hells bells, he'd told the truth, the whole truth and nothing but the truth, swelpme, all day long. Well, if they didn't believe him, they could go to the devil. And if that lawyer buzzard asked him a question on the way down to the livery stable, he'd really tell him a whopper - if he could think of one.

The question was forthcoming. "I understand you have some deep snows here in the winter, Slimber," Mr. Griggs said. "How deep do they get?"

The old man's eyes lit up. "Well, Mister," he said. "Some years worse than others. On a good year, maybe six feet on the level; bad years twice as much. That's not counting drifts that can be thirty feet high. People quit shoveling and just make tunnels to their gates. Not as bad here though, as in the Copper Country up the road. There they have snow so deep they have to keep crews working to keep the telephone wires from being buried."

Mr. Griggs pulled out the notebook and made an entry. "How do you keep the roads open?" he asked.

"We don't," said Slimber. "We just ski or snowshoe on top. We take the runners off our cutters and just slide along, toboggan-like behind the horse."

"But how do the horses ever get along in such deep snow?"

"On snowshoes, too, like us. Special round ones big around as this." Slimber made a big circle with his arms. "They soon learn how to spraddle their legs and walk on 'em easy as a man can. Course their legs are further apart anyway."

Mr. Griggs was gulping. "And the cold? It must get pretty cold up here," he said.

"Cold? That's God's truth," Slimber answered. "Stays in the twenty and thirty belows for months. That's why we make firewood all summer to keep from shivering all winter. And it gets colder than that, sometimes forty, fifty below. That's cold, Mister. If you spit when it's fifty below it pops in the air from freezing.

Mr. Griggs was impressed but thoughtful. "I don't know quite how to say it, but how do you er relieve yourself when the cold is so intense?"

"Well, said Slimber. "You just fill yer pants if you can't get to an outhouse. And if you can't wait to pee, you just let the tip of yer pecker out of your pants and hold it in both hands to keep it from freezing. Had a bad accident that way a year or two ago. Arnie Pelkie was in the bush on snowshoes when he couldn't hang on for another minute. Fifty-two below, it was, and with a strong wind, so Arnie straddles close behind a big tree to take his leak. Should have let it go down his leg inside his pants but he didn't, and you know what, his stream froze in the air and chained him to that there tree. If Okkari hadn't happened to come by to chop that icicle with his hand axe, Arnie would have been there till springs. He never did have any more kids after that."

A saintly smile came over Slimber's face. "Not bad," he said to himself, "Not bad."

THE ARTIST

One fine morning in July I was cutting across lots to see if I could persuade Mullu to explore Goochee Swamp with me. I wanted to know if it was true that a compass went crazy in that area. Just something to do when it was too bright for trout fishing. As I went through Marchand's barnyard I saw the old Frenchman talking to a stranger who had a suitcase beside him. "Ah, Cully," he called. "You come here, eh?. Zis man, he come from Chicago and need driver. You want to drive him, oui? He want find place for a cabin to build." I accepted eagerly. Might make a few dollars and it was better than fighting windfalls in that swamp. "How long will we be gone?" I asked the man.

"I don't know," he replied. "Perhaps just the morning. Perhaps all day. I plan to catch the evening train for Chicago but may stay a few days if I find what I want." I looked him over. A man about thirty, he was very stylishly dressed and topped by a straw hat. Every thing about him spelled city. While Marchand was hitching up old Maude to the buckboard I ran home to tell mother I might not be back for lunch, stuffed some cookies in my pocket, and returned.

As old Maude plodded down the hill, the man introduced himself. "I'm Carl Forster," he said. "I'm an artist, a painter. Up to now I've mainly done portraits and am sick of doing them. Want to try landscapes and such. Woodlands and water. But really what I want to do is to escape from the city and try a new life."

"How did you happen to pick Tioga?" I asked.

The man grinned. "Well I got a map," he said, "and decided to go as far north as the railroad would take me. So here I am riding behind an old horse along one of the most beautiful rivers I've ever seen and I've traveled widely both here and in Europe. Now all you have to do is to find me a Walden Pond so I can build a cabin and live a simple life free from all my past."

When I told him I'd read Thoreau's *Walden* and also his *A Week on the Concord and Merrimac River*, the artist was surprised and delighted. "Then you'll know what I'm seeking," he said. "But who are you? I've told you a bit about myself so it's your turn."

I answered that I was Cully Gage, the son of the town doctor, that I was sixteen years old and that my dad wanted me to go away to college but that I didn't want to at all. The thought that I might have to leave the forest and lakes and streams was hard to bear. Books were fine and I'd read a lot of them but going away to spend four years in classrooms and libraries didn't apeal to me a bit. Maybe I'd just take off, build me a shack up by Lake Superior and live off the land, hunting, fishing, and trapping.

"You are a kindred spirit, Cully, my friend, and I was lucky to find you," he said. "You probably know much that I must discover. All I know is that I've got to shed my old life as a snake sheds its skin. What was it Thoreau said? 'Simplicity, simplicity, simplicity. I've never known that.'" Out of his pocket he pulled a well-worn copy of Thoreau's Walden, hunting for a passage he'd underlined, then read it to me: "I went to the woods because I wished to live deliberately, to confront only the essential facts of life and see if I could learn what it had to teach, and not, when I came to die, discover I had not lived. I wanted to live deep and suck out all the marrow of life."

I interrupted. "He also said somewhere that most men live lives of quiet desperation. I don't want to live like that. I don't want to be famous or be rich. I just want to wander in the forest like a courier du bois or a mountain man living by my skills and wits." I felt a bit embarrassed talking that way to a grown man but found that he hadn't even been listening.

"Stop the horse!" he demanded. "Look at that! Look at that!" he exclaimed. We were in the middle of the plains where the forest fires had swept years before, in the center of a vast sea of white daisies, yellow buttercups, and orange paint brush with a few dark blueberry bushes thrown in. Mr. Forster cupped his hands, framed them, then peered out at the panorama. "Breathtaking! I must paint that. No more damned portraits. If I can..." He picked an Indian paintbrush to riffle its petals. "Burnt umber and..." He was talking to himself. Almost seemed to forget that Maude and I were there. Suddenly, after he had bent over and peered at the scene from between his legs, he snapped out of it. "I suppose you think I'm crazy doing that," he said, "But when I was in France studying painting, the master told me that only by looking at a landscape upside down could you see the true colors."

We stopped two more times, once so he could view a single white birch sapling from various distances, and then again when we came to Hansen's pool where the great granite hill plunges straight down into the river. There's a diagonal strip of red fedspar on the face of the cliff that contrasts with the blue-gray of the granite.

"Spectacular!" said Mr. Forster. "Spectacular! That I must paint too." He studied it for the longest time before noticing that Maude and I were getting restless. When finally he climbed back on the buckboard, he said, "Yes. This is where I live and paint. All I need is a Walden Pond where I can build a cabin."

I told him that up the road a little ways might be the place, that there was a little pond, maybe about five acres of it, on the south side of the road. It was spring fed, I told him, and its outlet was a little stream that ran under a culvert into the Tioga. There were a few trout in it too, I added, and asked him if he were a fisherman or hunter. No, he replied. He'd never caught a fish or fired a gun in his life. I wondered how the hell he'd ever make it through the winter.

When we got there, I took off Maude's bridle and put the halter on so the old gal could munch the grass along the road while we explored. It sure was a pretty place all right with a little clearing that overlooked both the pond and the river and a good view of the granite hills. Lots of spruce and balsam surrounded the opening and you could hear the gurgle of the stream down in the ravine. I sat on a rock in the clearing and ate a cookie as the artist prowled around exclaiming. When he returned he was ecstatic. "This is it. This is where I'll have my cabin. This is where I'll live the rest of my life! Let's see how big a cabin Thoreau built." He pulled out the book.

"If I remember right," I said, "It was ten by fifteen and cost him only twenty-eight dollars, but that was almost a hundred years ago. And he scrounged a lot of his building material including a thousand old bricks." Yes, I knew my Walden. After all I'd read it three times.

Mr. Forster had found the passage and corroborated the size and cost. He picked up a few rocks and placed them to show where the corners of a cabin about that size would be. "Yes," he said to himself. "A log cabin with a big window on this side overlooking the river, and another big window from which I can see my pond." I raised my eyebrows. "That would be OK for a summer cabin," I said, "but with all that glass you'd freeze to death in the winter. Thoreau didn't have that many windows in his cabin. And that will make it expensive too even if you'd build it yourself."

The artist laughed. "Oh no, I couldn't build anything. Surely there are men in Tioga who could. As for the expense, I don't care how much it costs. I inherited more money than I can ever use. Maybe that was my curse. Do you know of someone who could build it for me?"

I thought immediately of Mullu's father and told Mr. Forster about him. He was one of the best log butchers in the county. He'd built his own cabin, a fine one, two story and three bedrooms, and also several other cabins. At the moment too he was out of work and the haying was done so perhaps he might take the job. Not cheap but a real craftsman and absolutely honest. It would be hard to find a better person. But how about the land, I asked. You'll have to buy it from the owner.

"Of course," the artist replied. "I hadn't thought of that. How would I find the owner?" I suggested that the best way was to ask my father who was our township supervisor. He keeps the tax rolls and would have the information on the ledger," I said.

"Good!" replied the artist. "Wouldn't it be wonderful if I could buy the land and get someone to build the cabin before I go back to Chicago." I asked him if he wouldn't like to go further aong the river road to see some other possible places but he said no, that he'd found the place where he'd spend the rest of his life. We did stop at The Narrows where the river goes through a little gorge so he could watch the roaring rapids and the little islands of foam tumbling over the rocks.

"How can I capture that? How can I possibly?" he asked himself. Then opening his suitcase from under the seat he brought out a pad of heavy paper and some fat charcoal pencils to sketch me and Maude and the buckboard. He was a real artist all right. Just a few swift strokes and he had us right there on paper. Amazing! I hoped he might let me have it but no; he put the sketch back in the suitcase. Said he wanted to show it to someone in Chicago.

When we got back to Tioga, Mr. Forster asked me to take him to a restaurant and was shocked to find that we had none. "But where will I eat?" he asked. I thought of asking my mother to feed him but it was way past noon so I told him I'd drive him to Flynn's store where he could buy something for a picnic on the shore of Lake Tioga. Then we'd go back to find out from my father who owned the land and to see if Mr. Untilla would build the cabin.

Well, when he came out of the store, he'd bought bread, a pound of butter, a circle of bologna, cheese, milk, a can of peaches and a jacknife. I knew that jacknife well. I'd ogled it often because of all the little tools that were built into it, even scissors and a can opener. The latter would come in handy to open the peaches. We drove down to Lake Tioga and had our picnic on the rocky point where Beaver Dam Creek enters the big lake.

Again the artist was impressed by the beauty of our land, the long sandy beach on the east end of the lake, the islands in the distance, the huge hills that surrounded it. "I have found the place," he said over and over again. "Oh dear," he exclaimed, "I forgot to buy any cups or spoons or plates." No problem! From some poplar shoots I whittled out the utensils and then stripped some birch bark for plates and cups. That impressed him. "I have so much to lear," he said. He sure did. Why, I even had to tell him he could use his handkerchief for a napkin. How could he possibly make it through the winter living alone.?

When we drove back to town, I took him to my father's hospital. Dad was there and since there were no patients in the waiting room, I told him about the artist's needing to know who owned the land by the pond on the river road above the flats, because he was planning to build a cabin there to live in over the winter and beyond.

"Yes, I think I can find the owner," Dad said. "It's probably some big logging company but let's see." He opened up the big tax roll ledger and scrutinized a map. "No," he said. "That forty, the South $\frac{1}{4}$ of the Southeast $\frac{1}{4}$ of Section 32, Town 16 North, Range 14 West is owned by Pierre Rambeaux and the taxes haven't been paid for two years. He's probably planning on letting it revert to the state. You might be able to buy it for a song though you'll have to pay the back taxes. Cully, drive Mr. Forster down to Pierre's house and after the dickering is done, bring him up here so I can notarize the bill of sale."

Old Pierre was so surprised he almost forgot to dicker at all but they settled for five hundred dollars which Mr. Forster paid him in cash as soon as the sale had been witnessed by my mother and our hired girl. Mother was so charmed by the artist and his dream that she invited him for supper so he could stay with us until train time.

Now that the artist had his land, he had to find a builder. I took him over to see Mullu Untilla's father. When Mr. Forster described the cabin he wanted built, it was pretty evident that he didn't know much about cabins. Finally he pulled out his sketch pad and drew it. "Cully will show you where I want it built," he said. "I'll pay you whatever you charge and here's a thousand dollars earnest money." He pulled out ten one hundred dollar bills from a fat wallet.

Mullu's father hesitated. It sounded too good to be true. The man from Chicago wanted it done in two months which was really pushing it. He also wanted it furnished with table, chairs, bunk, and two stoves, one for cooking and one for heating.

"You'll also need a woodshed, an outhouse, and well. And storm windows or you'll never be able to stand the cold no matter how you fire up." Mullu's father was busy figuring costs. "And cut wood for the winter. What kind of logs you want for the walls? Cedar's best but cutting it would slow up work by a month. I've got seasoned red pine logs on a forty I own not far from your place. They make good cabin."

The artist said that red pine would be fine.

"What kind of roof? What kind of floor? Single or double bunk? You want cellar with trap door to keep potatoes and stuff from freezing?"

There were so many questions of that sort that finally the artist said, "Mr. Untilla, I know nothing of these things. You just build it as if it were your own and as if you were going to spend the rest of your life in it. I will pay you generously. I just want a cabin I can move into next September or October and start living and painting there. The two men shook hands.

I didn't have much chance to fish with Mullu that summer because he was always helping his father build the cabin and I was in school when Mr. Forster arrived about the middle of September. Mr. Untilla drove the artist with two trunks and a suitcase up to see the cabin. Utterly delighted with it, the artist paid Mullu's father five hundred dollars more than he asked. After the artist had been shown the outhouse and woodshed Mullu's father took him over to see the spring. He'd been unable to dig a well, he said, because two feet down there was only solid granite. Spring water was better anyway. It wouldn't freeze over like a well often did. If he needed more water for washing, he could haul it from the pond or the river. Mullu's mother had made pasties for them with an extra one for the artist's evening meal. The two men ate them, then Mr. Untilla left.

The cabin looked very bare after he was gone. The artist told me later that suddenly he felt catastrophically alone, completely helpless and overwhelmed. Most of the afternoon he just sat outside on one of the kitchen chairs reading Thoreau or walking down to the river to watch it flow by. As the shadows began to lengthen, he realized he should build a fire in the box stove and make up his bed. Never having built a fire before, he put the split wood on the bottom, then the kindling, and on top of them the birch bark. Untilla had given him a handful of matches and he used most of them before he got a blaze that would last.

Then the new stove and stovepipe smoked as they always do when the surface polish burns off and it took some time before he could figure out how to open the upper windows to let the smoke out. It was almost dark when the artist ate half of the other pasty down by the spring, drinking from it face down because he had no cup. When he returned, the cabin was black dark so he opened the door of the box stove to get enough light to make his bed with the silk sheets and cotton blanket from his trunk. No pillow. No mattress. Just hard boards. It was a long night.

When Mullu told me the artist had returned I hiked up the river road to visit him early the next morning. He was sure glad to see me. He had a notebook and was writing some things in it. "I'm making out a list of things I have to buy to furnish my cabin," he said. I looked at his list and there were only three items a pail, a cup, and a mattress. "Look, Cully," he said handing me his worn copy of Walden. "Thoreau had a bed, a table, a desk, a kettle, a skillet and a frying pan, three chairs, a wash bowl, two knives and forks, three plates, one cup, one spoon, a jug for oil and a japanned lamp. I'm sure I'll need a lot more but I can't figure out what they might be. Can you help me?"

I took his list and added these items: a dishpan, a tea kettle, coffee pot, frying pan, big saucepan for boiling potatoes, a kerosene lamp and oil for it, silverware for three.

"Why three?" he asked. "Thoreau says to simplify, simplify."

"Because you may have visitors drop in and you have to give them coffee and korpua or they'll think you're stuck up." I replied. "You'll also need some hay-wire, hammer and nails, and an axe and shovel," I added. "There's always a need for haywire, if only to make a hanger over the stove so you can dry your clothes, and you'll need a shovel to dig a garbage pit and to clean out the spring."

"Yes, one about four feet deep and square, so the bears won't raid the cabin. Keep the stuff covered with dirt. And three cups and a paring knife and a butcher knife and maybe a pancake turner. You can turn a pancake with two knives but a pancake turner is better." I explained.

"I've never turned a pancake in my life," the artist said. "Indeed I've never cooked a meal for myself in my life." He explained that his family always had a cook and servants, and that after he was on his own he always ate in restaurants or had room service sent up. I find myself really helpless, Cully," he said, "and I'm scared. Nothing in my life has prepared me for this. Graduating from Harvard cum laude never taught me how to make coffee...."

I interrupted. "Yes, you'll have to buy a coffee pot, a teapot. Oh, I've already got those down on the list. What else? Some bowls for soup though you could use a cup. Better get two pails, not just one. And some towels. And soap."

"How about clothing and bedding? I asked. Explaining that one trunk contained only his artist's supplies, he opened the other. It held three changes of underwear but no long johns, a sweater, two fine linen shirts, some fine handkerchiefs, some books and candles. Mr. Forster pointed to the bunk. "All the blankets and sheets are there but they sure didn't keep me warm last night," he said. "I'll need to buy some more but what should I get?" I told him he needed two woolen blankets, a heavy comforter, some winter underwear, heavy woolen pants and socks, and a mackinaw. Oh, yes, also a slicker or some other kind of rain gear. And boots, I added, looking at his fancy store shoes. He'd need some clompers like I wore, with rubber bottoms.

"But what I need most, after that terrible night," the artist said, "is a good mattress. My bones still ache. Do you think we could find one down at Flynn's store?" I doubted it. He might have to take the train to Ishpeming to get some of the things.

"What food supplies will I need to buy?" he asked. "Thoreau had a list of the food he lived on for eight months. Oh yes, here it is on page 57: rice, molasses, rye meal, Indian meal, pork, flour, sugar, lard, apples, potatoes, one pumpkin, one watermelon, salt.' Of course he also had a garden."

"Well, let's make a list," I said. "what do you usually have for breakfast in Chicago?"

"Oh, nothing much," he replied. "Always fruit juice or fruit in season - melon, grapefruit, strawberries. Then a croissant and coddled egg. Perhaps a rasher of bacon, toast and marmalade."

Fruit in season? I wrote "apples" on my list. "What's a coddled egg?" I asked. "How do you coddle an egg? Fondle it?"

He grinned. "I don't really know," he answered. "It comes in its own little cup and you have to unscrew the lid. Then you salt and pepper it and dip it out with a small spoon."

"And what's a croissant? You won't find any at Flynn's store."

It was a kind of French pastry, he explained, crescent shaped. I told him the closest he could come to that was a chunk of korpua. I didn't query him further, just made up the list myself. "Apples, bread, butter, korpua, eggs, slab of bacon, coffee." The artist said that he preferred coffee au lait with a spoonful of sugar. OK. "Milk, condensed milk, sugar, salt and pepper." Lunch? He liked consomme, a salad, asparagus spears on toast or a sandwich. "Pea soup, two cans," I wrote. "butter, lard, pork and beans, corned beef, cheese, potatoes, a rutabaga, a cabbage, ketchup, pancake flour, syrup, corn meal, yeast and baking powder. Oh yes, some toilet paper too."

We added two items on our way back to town. A strong wind kept blowing the straw hat off his head and after a mile or two he began to limp a bit. "You need a cap with ear laps," I told him, "and some boots or clompers like I wear. Those shoes will never hold up on these stones and gravel." He agreed but forgot to write them down on the list.

"How far is my cabin from Tioga?" he asked. "Thoreau had his about two miles from town." I told him three or four miles.

When we got to Marchand's livery stable I asked the old man if we could have his dray wagon with the long box because Mr. Forster had to haul a lot of supplies. Sure, the old man said, but we'd have to have Maude again. While they were hitching up I ran home to ask Dad if we could have two of the old hospital mattresses he had stored in the back room after the mine closed. "They won't be very soft," Dad replied. "They're filled with wooden shavings. Be sure to get ones without any mouseholes in the ticking." We picked them up on our way to the store and they fit just right in the wagon box. Smelled a little musty though.

When Mr. Forster gave Mr. Flynn the list, the storekeeper gasped. "That'll cost you over a hundred dollars," he said. The artist didn't bat an eye so Flynn and his clerk and I went to work collecting the stuff. No, Mr. Flynn didn't have any comforters or candle holders but he had everything else. Quite a load! The artist also bought some steaks for supper since I'd told him that after I'd brought the horse and wagon back I'd hike to the cabin to spend the night with him and help him get organized. He was very grateful.

When we got to the cabin I helped him unload by the road and showed him where to dig a hole below the spring where he could put a pail to keep the milk and butter cold, then drove Maude back to Tioga.

When I told mother I was going back to spend the night she wasn't sure it was a good idea. I tried to explain how helpless the man was. Dad came in while I was telling her and said, " He'll never make it. He'll be out of here by Christmas." I had the same thought but hoped it was wrong. "Anyway," I said, "He's paying me five dollars a day for helping him and that's not hay." Dad thought it was too much. I put a woolen blanket and a sweater in my packsack, took a bunch of cookies from the pantry and was on my way.

When I got to the new cabin I figured it was about four thirty or five o'clock. Maybe I'd have time to make him a balsam bed to put under that hard mattress. The artist was sitting outside in a chair sketching a big spruce and when I entered the cabin, I knew why. Lord, I could hardly enter it. Mr. Forster had hauled all the stuff from the road but had just piled it at random in the cabin. He said again that he'd felt overwhelmed. Didn't know where to put the stuff. Well, I got the two trunks, put them side by side under the east window, and put a mattress on top. That cleared out enough space to walk around in. When I told the artist to put the potatoes and rutabaga and cabbage in the cellar, he had to be shown where the ring to the trap door was. He'd forgotten he had a cellar. I set him to work driving nails into the logs behind the cookstove to hold the skillets, pans and stuff but then had to show him how to hold a hammer and how to start the nail with short taps before driving it in. Lord, he was clumsy. I also had to straighten most of his nails so the pans wouldn't slip off. To keep him out of my hair while I built some shelves from boards I found in the woodshed, I asked him to peel some potatoes for supper. He didn't know how to peel a potato as I discovered later. He'd cut the potatoes in little chunks first and was whittling away the skin. So I showed him.

Finally I got the place organized so you could move around with the canned stuff on the shelves, and the clothing hung up on the nails. To keep him busy while I made him a balsam bed, I told the artist how to make a cooking fire outside between two logs so we could have coals for the steaks and to start boiling the potatoes and to make a potato masher out of one of the split wood in the woodshed. I figured he'd never get done peeling those little chunks of potatoes so we might as well mash them skins and all.

Between loads of balsam tips, I supervised his fire building. At least he'd learned to put the birch bark on the bottom and the kindling above it but the split wood he'd brought from the woodshed was way too large so I had to show him how to split them in finer lengths. Hd never used an ax. Didn't even know how to put the stick of wood upright against a chunk. Didn't know how to hit it so the blade would angle just at the moment of contact. Didn't know how to extricate the axe when it got stuck. But he learned and by the time I had his balsam bed done and the mattress atop it he had some good coals between the two logs with potatoes boiling and apples cooking in the other pan. I had to make the potato masher myself and teach him how to sear the steaks and salt them. He wanted to eat by candlelight but since Mr. Flynn had no candleholders, I got a couple of Indian slates (a lichen) from a yellow birch, made holes in them, showed him how to turn the lighted candle upside down to fill the hole with hot wax, then put it in the hole until it was held firm. It was dark when the food was done but we had a fine meal by candlelight before going to bed. Even then, I had to show him how to roll up his sweater to make the pillow that Flynn didn't have. I slept on the mattress on top of the trunks and he in the bunk after demonstrating how to blow out a candle or a kerosene lamp by cupping your hands over the chimney or flame. He sure slept well and so did I.

The next morning we had applesauce (fruit in season), pancakes, bacon and coffee. No croissants! I had to show him how to make boiled coffee, how to have it turn over, pull it aside, let it come to a boil again, then put a dollop of water to settle the grounds. The artist sure had trouble slicing the bacon off the slab. Until I showed him how to slice along the rind, then cut, he had been sawing on that rind with the butcher knife in vain. He didn't know that you had to pierce two holes in the condensed milk can before it would pour. He didn't know that when you stirred pancake batter you always left a few small lumps. Hell, he didn't even know how to crack an egg. Harvard cum laude! The first pancakes he cooked were terrible but with some instruction about watching for the bubbles he finally managed to flip them without getting them in his hair. It was a good breakfast. Mr. Forster said he'd never had a better cup of coffee even in the Waldorf Astoria.

The water was hot in the teakettle and in the reservoir of the wood range so we did the dishes. The man didn't know that you rinsed them in fresh water afterwards before drying. Drying? No towels. Again he was helpless. I got one of his five bath towels from the trunk and cut it to make two dishtowels and two dish rags. Where should he put the dishwater? "Throw it out the door," I said. Before I left I told him how to make a salad dressing for his cabbage: Mix some ketchup with a beaten egg and a little milk, then salt and pepper. And cut the cabbage fine. I had him practice using the little can opener on his jacknife so he could have soup for lunch, then demonstrated how he would have to turn the key to unwind the top of the corn beef cans. "Cut the slices about this thick and fry them slowly till they're brown on top," I told him.

He hated to see me go after he paid me ten dollars and I started out of the door. "I hope you'll come back to see me when you can, Cully," he said. I told him I might be able to make it after school the next Thursday if we didn't have basketball practice but I would be sure to come up Saturday to see how he was doing. He walked with me about a mile down the river road before turning back.

I was able to get away that next Thursday afternoon after school and found the artist frying some ham and sliced potatoes for supper even though I got there about five o'clock. Very glad to see me, he seemed to have a terrible urge to talk. He was all right. He'd dug the garbage pit and had to show me both it and his blisters. Would I stay for supper? He'd cooked enough for both, on the chance I might show up. He'd had a little accident, pouring kerosene on a slow-starting fire in the cookstove. Singed his arm when it blew off the lids. He was now eating when he felt like it and had forgotten to have lunch that day. The balsam bed was heavenly. He'd slept soundly except when something gnawed at the door early one morning. (I told him it was probably a porcupine.) Some creature had been chewing the toilet paper in the outhouse. (Probably a mouse.) He'd taken a swim off the sandy beach east of where he got the wash water, soaped good, and swam again. Terribly cold but exhilerating. How do you cut a rutaga? (With an ax, first.) The salad dressing on the cabbage was fine but he hungered for vinegar or pickle juice and also for sweets. Bread and butter with sugar on it was excellent.

I asked him if he'd done any painting. "No," he replied, "I did try some water colors trying to get the green for that pine out in front of the cabin."

"It's a spruce, a white spruce," I said.

"Whatever it is, I am determined to capture it. I'll probably have to use oils."

On the way up the river road I'd noticed that the trees were beginning to show the color changes, the reds and scarlets of fall. "Why not paint them?" I asked.

"Too garish. Too overwhelming. If I can capture that pine, I mean spruce tree, that would be a supreme achievement. But I'm really too busy just surviving to have time to paint. By the time I've made my bed, had my breakfast, done the dishes and tried to clean the place it's time for lunch. I walked around the pond yesterday and it took all afternoon. Oh, Cully, do you think you could clear a path around it? It's awfully hard walking in all that brush and broken trees except in the marsh on the far side."

We went down to see the pond. It sure was beautiful but the brush around it and the windfalls, especially among the cedars, made it in spots almost impenetrable. So I told him, no, that I alone couldn't do it on a weekend or two but that if he would hire two of my friends, Mullu and Fisheye, we might be able to clear a good path in two days. That was fine, he said. He didn't care how much it cost. Just wanted to be able to walk around his Walden pond and bathe himself in beauty.

After we had our early supper, I said it was time to go if I were to get home before dark. This time he gave me, not only a five dollar bill, but a hundred dollar one with a list of things he said he needed. "Bring your friends up and the supplies on the buckboard Saturday and pay Marchand whatever he asks." After I looked at the list I told him I thought we could pack it in.

Mullu and Fisheye were tickled pink when I told them they could get five dollars a day for cutting brush up at the artist's cabin and after they saw the list they agreed to help bring it in their packsacks too. Here was the artist's list after only five days in camp: clothesline, vinegar, dipper, ladle, scissors, needles and thread, tablespoons, broom. (I told the artist he could make a broom like the Finns always did but he said no, he wanted a real broom, oh yes, and a dustpan too), something to sharpen the knife and axe, a serrated knife to cut bread, more bread and milk, four steaks and a pasty if I could buy one (I told him no, that all our families made them but not for sale.) More soup, a different kind if possible. Cookies and maybe candy; another pail and another bigger frying pan. Some pickles. And especially a pillow if I could get one. And some wine. A knitted cap he could pull over his ears.

No wine, I said. Higley only sold beer and whiskey and he wouldn't let a kid like me inside the door of his saloon. As for the knitted cap, I didn't think Flynn would have one. Put a bandana handkerchief over your head. Your straw hat looks silly up here. I might be able to find a cap but I don't know your size. He said it was 7¼.

Well we got all the stuff although I had to get the pillow from my mother, and Mullu got a pasty from his. Up the river road we went carrying our heavy packs and me holding a broom. Sure looked silly in bird season. Oh yes, Fisheye had also swiped a bottle of wild black cherry wine from his cellar, so we had everything on the artist's list.

We found him outside with his easel set up sketching the outline of that spruce tree but he dropped everything and helped us unpack and went with us to the pond where we started clearing the path. Mullu had brought up an axe and a bucksaw and Fisheye had a hatchet so the work went swiftly. Mr. Forster was so fascinated by the bucksaw and how it went so easily through one of the cedar windfalls, we let him try it. It took him some time to learn to hold the saw frame straight and not to keep pressing down. Also he was surprised to find that by bending over a bush it was easier to cut off at the base. By five o'clock we were finished and, because we hadn't eaten anything since morning, those steaks and potatoes sure were good. Afterward, the artist sketched the three of us sitting on a log, paid us each ten dollars and bought Mullu's bucksaw for another ten because a new one only cost eight dollars. We felt so rich we built him a sawbuck behind the cabin and hauled some cedar logs up from the swamp so he could make kindling. Again we had to show him how to split off the slabs and make the fine stuff. Again he walked part way home with us.

I only visited the artist two or three times the last of October and early in November. He was doing all right. Seemed happy and content. The only trouble he'd had was keeping the fire going all night in the box stove. He said that usually he had to get up four or five times so I showed him how to bank the fire with ashes before he went to bed and to be sure he had a green log on top. He'd been doing a lot of painting as well as sketching and had a wonderful picture of the big spruce on canvas. When I told him it was magnificent, he disagreed. "No, Cully, it's not right. I haven't been able to capture that glint on the needles, that sheen." He showed me a pencil sketch of a deer and a half-grown fawn that had posed for him one evening at the edge of the clearing. He sure could draw.

When I visited him again in early November after I'd had my belly full of hunting partridge, ducks and rabbits, he was working on a canvas, trying to paint a spruce branch with some cones on it. "Too cold to paint outside," he said. He'd done a washing which hung kitty-corner from one end of the cabin to the other. He'd hung it outside the day before but it froze overnight. He said he had washed the clothes, underwear, shirts and socks, in the river but wouldn't do it again. Too cold. He told me that Fisheye and Mullu had been up to cut some more wood for the winter and showed me proudly how much kindling he'd sawed and split. No, he didn't need anything. I refused to take any money for checking on him. When I left I felt that he might really make it through the winter.

We did see him in town occasionally because he usually walked in to buy groceries or to take a sauna at Mullu's house on Saturday afternoons, or to get or post his mail. Once, while he was waiting for the mail to be disturbed (distributed), among the men there was old Pete Ramos. The artist became so fascinated by the old bugger's craggy face, he paid him five dollars to let him sketch it. A perfect likeness, it even showed the wart on the west side of the old drunk's nose. Then he posted it up on the bulletin board along with the other posters of men wanted for murder and other crimes. Our people in Tioga got a kick out of that and were proud to have a real artist in town - even if he did live way out in the bush. As for old Pete, he was proud too. I don't know how many days he came to the post office to see his picture.

Once the artist went to Ishpeming on the train and when he returned with a comforter, more socks and some wine, he asked me to teach him how to drive old Maude up to the cabin. No problem! He did everything wrong at first, trying to steer the old horse by pulling on the reins when he didn't need to. Finally Maude stopped and looked back to see what the hell was going wrong, so I showed him to let her go with the reins limp, how to slap her rump when she slowed down too much, and how to swear at her in French like old Marchand did.

I guess the last time I went to his cabin was about the middle of November, just before deer season. Mother had invited him to stay for supper. She liked the artist a lot. Said he was a real gentleman. By that time it was dark even at five o'clock but the artist said he'd love to have a home cooked meal and wouldn't have any trouble walking back under the stars.

But there weren't any stars by the time we finished supper. Instead a real blinger of a blizzard hit us. High wind and snow coming down so thick you couldn't see a foot in front of you. We get sudden storms like that in the U.P. Anyway Dad insisted he spend the night with us. He could sleep with me in the big brass bed and head for camp in the morning. It was a very pleasant evening. Mother played Chopin on the piano; Dad told some of his gory medical tales; and the artist described his experiences living alone. No he wasn't at all lonely. A raven flew over his clearing twice a day; a red squirrel was always around; he'd tamed a couple of Canadian Jays to eat bread out of his hand; occasionally a hunter would drop in for coffee and korpua. No, he wasn't lonely a bit. Thoreau was right!

His only problem, he said, was that he was having a hard time doing landscapes, especially trying to capture a big spruce tree in front of the cabin. He was a pretty good portrait painter, he said, and had studied landscapes in Italy, but that spruce tree was sure hard to get right.

Dad told him that it would be a different spruce tree when he saw it again, that it would be loaded with snow. Oh, I forget most of the conversation but it was fun to listen to. The artist told us he was thirty years old, the same age that Thoreau had been when he went to Walden Pond. He said that it was difficult to live as Thoreau did. He'd been trying to bake bread his way but the results were disastrous. Mother gave him her recipe, the one using potato water. Finally we went to bed with the wind howling in the shutters. Mr. Forster was not a very good bed partner. Kept tossing around probably because he missed that balsam bed and the hard hospital mattress.

The next morning we had over a foot of snow on the level and it was still snowing so Dad told me to hitch old Billy to the cutter, and drive the artist back to the cabin. He gave him a pair of our snowshoes and told me to teach him how to walk on them. I put a lot of Dad's Chicago Tribunes in the packsack so he could read them or use them for a fire if the birch bark ran out or to clean his lamp chimney.

On the way I let Mr. Forster drive and he did fine although Billy was feeling his morning oats. The cabin was very cold, of course, and the artist couldn't understand why, after we built a fire in both stoves, I insisted on keeping the door open for awhile. Fresh air always warms better than stale air, I told him. I helped him haul water from the pond and said that if it froze over he could make a hole with the axe or get water from the river or spring. He was sure having a hard time on the snowshoes but finally learned how to swing his legs so one of them wouldn't sit on top of the other. It was still snowing hard when I drove home.

After that I didn't go up again but saw him several times when he walked to town. He was fortunate because Silverthorne and Company were logging way up at the headquarters of the Tioga and kept the river road plowed out that winter. Anyway he came to town every week for his necessaries or mail and sometimes he dropped in at our house. Once he gave my father the sketch he'd drawn of the deer and fawn, and he told me he thought that at last he'd really captured that spruce tree covered with snow. He never said paint, always capture.

Annie, our postmistress, let the word leak out that when he'd first come to

Tioga all the mail he got or sent were letters to or from a law firm but that lately he'd been sending letters, sometimes two at a time, to a Simone Bouregard in Chicago. Never a Miss or Mrs., just the name, and he'd also been getting mail from someone in a woman's writing on very fancy stationery. Romance? I sure didn't know. The artist had never said a word about any of his past relationships.

But we were surprised when we learned that on a December morning a beautiful tall woman dressed in expensive furs had got off the morning train from Chicago, to be greeted by the artist, and whisked away in Marchand's cutter pulled by old Maude. "Why there must have been thirty or forty mink skins in that coat," someone said who had seen her. "And she had a fur cap and tall boots with fur on them too." All we really knew is that he brought her back that afternoon and she took the evening train for Chicago.

Two days later the artist also took that train and we never saw him again. After the breakup next spring I hiked up to his cabin and found it just as he'd left it. No one had been there so far as I could see. There was even old coffee in the pot. No note of explanation. His paintings were still there but the fine one of the spruce tree was smeared and crisscrossed with paint. That was all.

We hoped that he might return that spring or summer but he never did, then or ever. Was it that he had to go back to that beautiful woman and an easier, less lonely life? Or was it that he finally realized he would never be able to capture the spruce tree? There are a lot of mysteries in the U.P. and that was one of them. Anyway, Tioga had an artist once.

TO MY GRANDSON

Dear Jim: Your Uncle Tim and I will pick you up at six-thirty Thursday morning for the long trip north so you'd better have your breakfast and have your stuff ready to go by that time. I'm sorry your father couldn't make it this year but I'm glad you can take his place. You will be the fourth generation of Gage men to hunt deer in the forest around the lakes that bear our name. I say "men" because, although you're only sixteen, we will treat you like a man, not a boy, and will expect that you'll act like one.

For example, when we get there the cabin will probably be cold and damp. We'll build a big fire in the fireplace while you chop a hole in the ice of the lake to get two pails of water for drinking, dishes, or priming the pump. You may wonder why we will open the door and windows when we build the fire. We do so because fresh air heats up faster than stale air. That's just one of the many things you'll learn at deer camp. After getting the water, chop a lot of cedar kindling and some small wood. Put these beside the big woodbox, not in it. Then haul in the big chunks of hard maple until the woodbox is full and has a heap on it. During our stay at the cabin, getting wood and water will be your primary chores.

But there will be others too. When the alarm clock goes off at five-thirty you will hop out of your sleeping bag pronto, build up the fire and make the coffee. To do the latter, you put in eight level tablespoons of coffee along with eight cups of water into the pot. Watch it closely when it begins to boil, let the grounds turn over, then take it off the fire for a minute, then put it back on the fire for a second short boiling. After that, plunge in a half cup of water to settle the grounds and set the pot on the back of the stove. We'll drink a lot of coffee up here and it's your job to make sure there's always coffee in the pot when we come in from hunting. Your final job is to wash and rinse the dishes. We'll dry them and put them away, do the camp cleaning, keep the fire going all night, and occasionally help you with your duties.

Why do so many men feel that ancient urge to go deer hunting each year? According to the papers there will be more than 700,000 of us in the woods on opening day. It is certainly no longer just for meat though when I was a boy in the U.P. venison was vital in our making it through the winter. Not now! For the money I will spend on this expedition I could fill my freezer to overflowing with the best cuts of choice beef or pork. Venison is good, but not that good and I sure had my fill of it when I was growing up.

No, there must be some other reason that impels us to leave all the conveniences of home to freeze on a stump or shiver on the trails for hours on end. In part we hunt deer for the escape from all responsibility, from our wives and work. It provides an opportunity to share man talk and male companionship, a chance to play and be carefree.

But there is something more. Deep in our genes, or whatever, there is a primeval urge to hunt and kill which has been transmitted since the earliest times in the human race. Men have always been hunters. Certainly we Gages have been. The first Gage came to America in the late 1600's when the land was all wilderness. Successive generations of Gages moved gradually westward, always at the edge of the forest, until the 1850's when they made a long hard trek by covered wagon and on foot to southwestern Michigan. I remember my grandfather, Arza Gage, telling about how on that journey his Aunt Patience and mother cooked pancakes for some Indians until the men came back from hunting, dragging a deer. He said that the women made the pancakes small so they could gain time. He also told me that when he was a teamster in the logging camps up by Saginaw, he always carried a rifle in his wagon to shoot any deer he could get because that was the only meat the lumberjacks ever had except salt pork. So he was a deer hunter too, like you.

My own father, your great grandfather, Dr. John Gage, never missed a deer season until late in his eighties and he always got a deer or two or three others for his hunting cronies who didn't hunt as hard or long as he did. Arising before daybreak and with only an apple and a sandwich in his pocket for lunch, he'd hunt until dark. I understand from your father that you will be using my father's rifle. That's good. Your great grandfather would have liked that. Take good care of it.

As for me, in my own eighties, I have no urge any more to shoot another deer. I've shot my share. Indeed I felt bad when I shot the last one and every footstep I took when dragging it back to camp was a penance. But I still have that primitive urge to hunt even though I won't shoot. I love the feel of a gun under my arm as I walk this forest I know so well with every sense on immediate alert. I love to read the animal tracks in the clean snow. The woods in winter is another world from that in summer. When the sun lightens up the openings between firs shaggy with white snow it can be like walking in a fairyland. Even as I write this I feel the old excitement welling up within me. Yes, I sure have the ancient urge.

On the first morning after we've had a fine breakfast I'll take you up the camp road a ways, then to your first sitting place just a bit north of a good deer trail. It will still be too dark to see to shoot and you should sit there watching the trail until it's light and you can't bear sitting another moment. Then you should start walking east and roughly parallel to the trail until you hit an old logging road. I suggest that you turn right (south) on it for about a quarter of a mile, then circle back by going west until you hit our camp road again. This area is my favorite deer hunting territory as it was my father's and I don't think you can get very lost unless you go north. *Don't* go north! If you do you'll come out on Lake Superior thirty or more miles away. If you go east far enough, you'll finally come out on the new road along Dishno Creek. If you go south, you'll also hit that road eventually, and if you go west, you'll come out on our camp road. So you shouldn't get lost even if you can't backtrack because the wind has covered your tracks. Just go east, or south or preferably west and you'll get back to camp. It's wise, however, to occasionally check your compass to see which way you're going or to know which way you've been coming from.

As you sit or stand watching for deer, don't take quick glances but rather let your eyes sweep across the terrain, almost as though you were using binoculars. If you see anything that looks remotely like a deer or deer head focus on that until you're sure it isn't. Also, look back on your trail because sometimes a curious deer may follow it. Above all, try to see the lay of the land, the hills, gulleys, swamps and little streams. Look for landmarks that you can recognize again. There's a lone big hemlock on a steep hill that you should spot, a large arch made by a maple sapling, a cascade of big boulders where a bear once made its den. On the north side of one of the hills is a large stand of beautiful white birch. Maybe you'll find my throne, a big hollow pine stump at the end of a ridge. I shot a deer once from that throne.

Let me suggest before you move from you spot that you practice targeting your rifle. Pick out some target, a stump, or sapling, then bring up your rifle, aim at it and squeeze the trigger. I hope I don't have to tell you that you should have the safety on. It really helps your coordination when you actually see a buck. If you don't practice you may have trouble lining up the sights.

And remember to listen. At times the sharp crack of a broken branch may mean that a deer has broken it. That's why you should step over, not on such a branch as you walk. But listen too to all the other sounds, to the croak of ravens flapping overhead, to the sliver cats. That's what we call trees that groan as they rub together. If you hear a deer snort, freeze. He's got your scent and will be circling you.

Most of the winter birds, except the ravens, are silent creatures. Even the blue jays rarely screech. I like the Canadian jays best because they're curious and friendly and very appreciative of a crumb of korpua or bit of apple as they show by twittering. I once had one perch on my gun barrel. People of the U.P. call them whiskey jacks and claim that they are the reincarnation of dead lumberjacks.

Red squirrels can be a nuisance when you're hunting. It's not bad if they are merely using their single ratchety calls but when they sit in a tree above where you're standing and chatter excitedly,you'd better move on. Every deer within a mile will be able to locate you.

As you follow a trail or cut cross-country note the various animal tracks you encounter so you can tell us about them at Happy Hour. I'd guess that you'd better put a pad of paper and pencil in your pocket with the apple and korpua so we can help you identify your sketches. Fox tracks go in a straight line usually; the Y-shaped rabbit tracks show they are leaping. A partridge leaves a thick trail of webbed marks. A bobcat has the padded prints of a house cat, only larger. A bear track looks like a stubby human hand. You may even come across a moose track, three times as large as any deer. If you see a moose, don't even point your rifle at it. Any man from the U.P. would beat you senseless if you shot one. They airlifted a lot of them from Canada and let them go not four miles from our lake and we want the herd to get established. I've not seen any moose yet but I've seen their tracks by the beaver dam.

You may hear some far-away shots. Remember to tell us about them and when they occurred because they usually mean that the deer are moving at that time. Generally speaking, the best times to see a deer are from early in the morning until about ten o'clock, then again from four until dark but once I shot a buck at noon. Tim and I usually come back to camp about ten o'clock for coffee and I take a nap in the afternoon until two.

I don't think you'll see any hunter in your territory. Most of them prefer to hunt the plains south of Ishpeming or Republic where there are many more deer. To put it bluntly, there aren't very many deer around our lakes. That's why they planted the moose so near us, to keep them from catching the brain worm that deer have but are invulnerable to. Nevertheless, as you will discover, there are deer near our lakes and their relative scarcity just makes the challenge all the greater. You'll see fresh tracks every day. Actually I'm always amazed when I've shot a buck. The odds are all in its favor. This is big country and the chances that you and the buck will have your trails intersect at exactly the same instant at a particular spot in that vast expanse of forest are really very low. Yet most years we get our bucks. If we don't, no matter. We'll get one next year. The fun is in the hunting, not the kill.

I suppose you're wondering if you might get buck-fever. I would doubt it. You've hunted before and shot pheasants and rabbits. When that buck is in your sights you'll shoot straight. And be back at the cabin by five o'clock so we won't worry.

No I don't think there's any real possiblity that you'll get really lost but if you do or if you are injured so you can't walk, then give the following signal. Shoot twice in quick succession, then count slowly to sixty, then fire two more shots, then wait about a minute more, then fire two more. We'll find you, so sit on a log until we get there. By the way, be sure to take a small plastic garbage bag in your pocket to serve as a dry-ass. Even though you scrape the snow off a sitting log you'll get a band of wetness across your rump unless you have one.

Now to the deer hunting itself. My father repeatedly told me to try to walk as slowly as possible and either to sit quietly without moving or to stand alongside a tree. And never to make a quick movement! Once he walloped me for moving my head before moving my eyes and told me if I saw a walking deer to bring my rifle up slowly not quickly. Deer can see movement though their eyesight is not as keen as their senses of smell or hearing. He also insisted that I always try to keep upwind when I chose a sitting or standing place. Usually the wind up here is from the west or northwest but not always, so check it. Deer tend to travel upwind.

None of us Gages have ever been long sitters even though we know that this is the best way to get a deer. Most of the Finns up here can sit all day along a deer trail until one comes along. I just can't sit so long and never could even when I was younger. Fifteen minutes or perhaps half an hour is all I can stand or rather sit and then I have to get moving, always wanting to see what's over the next hill. My main method of hunting is to prowl through the woods looking and listening until I find a fresh track. This I follow, not right on the trail because deer often keep looking back at where they've been, but some distance parallel with it, first on one side of the trail, then on the opposite side. If the deer is making long leaps (I once measured one that was nineteen feet) I don't bother because it will be half a mile away before I catch up to him but it the deer is feeding as evidenced by its wandering around and nipping off the tips of maple brush and I don't cross its trail again, I sit or stand in wait, and have often gotten my buck that way.

How can I tell if the track is a buck or doe? I really haven't been able to determine this except that very large bucks seem to leave sharper points in their hoofprints than do the does. Usually it doesn't matter because often a buck will be following the doe anyway, so if you see a doe be sure to wait ten or fifteen minutes. And look for fresh beds or scrapes on saplings that seem new, or for oval black deer turds that are still steaming. The deer will be very near. How can you tell a fresh track from an old one? I know but it's hard to put into words. I'll have to show you. If there are granular bits of snow in the track it's not new.

You've seen deer in the summer when fishing up here but their rich brown coats are replaced in the winter by gray ones, so look for gray, not brown. Often they'll appear like grey ghosts, so quietly do they present themselves. In thick brush all you may see is a head and neck so look for these too. Most of the deer you'll see will be walking, or running with their white tails held high. Sometimes if you whistle sharply a running deer will stop, trying to see where the sound comes from. Only rarely will you see a deer standing still. If you do he will be watching you.

Of course, the first thing you do when you see a deer is to look for horns. We Gages have never shot a doe or fawn and you'd better not be the first one to do so. Any deer with antlers is fair game. This holds true for spikehorns too but the prongs must be at least three inches long to be legal. These prongs are often hard to see but if you have any smidegon of doubt don't shoot. Better to have a spikehorn get away than to shoot a doe.

Where should you aim? If the buck is sideways to you, aim for a spot right behind the upper front shoulder. Some beginners after that first shot will lower their rifles waiting for the deer to fall. A veteran hunter will shoot again as quickly as possible. If the buck has not dropped in its tracks, go immediately to where you saw it and look for blood spots. If you find some substantial ones, wait about fifteen minutes before following the trail so it will lie down. Most deer, even if mortally wounded, will run a short distance before they fall. If, when you find it, and it is still living but unable to move, shoot it again in the neck to end its suffering. You may not want to do this but you must.

If you find occasional blood spots but no dead deer you must follow the trail. We Gages always stay on the trail of a wounded deer until no more blood signs are seen and we know that the wound was superficial. Your great Grandfather once kept trailing a wounded deer until dark, came back to camp for a flashlight and a blanket and returned after midnight but he got his buck.

Where do you shoot if the buck is coming right toward you? You aim for the upper part of the chest, just below the neck. Some hunters will shoot randomly at a running deer or shoot it in the side or hind end. We Gages don't because there's too much chance of merely wounding it and a lot of the meat will be spoiled anyway. The best way to get a running buck is to note which way it's going and then aim ahead of it. When it comes into your sights, squeeze the trigger. Yes, squeeze it; don't pull it. And after you've shot, put the safety back on.

If the buck is on a hillside higher than you, there's always a tendency to undershoot, so hold your rifle so that all of your front sight is in view. Conversely, if the buck is downhill from you, draw a fine bead on the front sight so you won't overshoot.

After you've killed your first deer, you'd better come right back to camp. We will have heard you shoot and will be ready to help you clean it, or rather to tell you what to do. It's a bloody business and not difficult but there's a knack to it. First you must lay the deer on its back with its head higher than the legs. Then you'll have to slit around the balls, then up the belly to the sternum, the bottom of the rib cage. After that you'll cut the windpipe and diaphragm and spill the entrails on the ground, saving the liver. Then we'll help you drag your buck back to the cabin and hoist it up to hang from the buck pole on the woodshed for all to admire.

That evening during Happy Hour while supper's cooking the three uf us will be sitting in the big chairs before the fire munching on crackers covered with the smoked whitefish we picked up at Naubinway. We may even give you a shot glass containing diluted whiskey which will taste awful and we will raise our glasses to the latest member of the clan to get his buck. We will want to know every minute detail about what happened, where you first saw the buck, your feelings, how you targeted it, how it reacted, oh, everything. It is a tale you will tell many times so get it straight. Some day you will tell it to the next Gage, your son.

MY ISLAND

For almost sixty years I had an island on a hidden unnamed lake in the U.P. I discovered it when I was nineteen while roaming the granite hills north of Tioga in search of gold. Yes, there is gold in them thar hills, gold as well as hundreds of other minerals including uranium. Today just west of Ishpeming a gold mine is still going full tilt on a site where, long ago, the Ropes and Michigan gold mines yielded millions of dollars worth of gold—and even more from the pockets of their shareholders.

Over and over again, as a boy, I had heard the tales. Jim Bedford, station agent at Humboldt, on his day off had gone trout fishing on a creek that empties into the Escanaba River. On his way back he cut cross-country and got lost. As he came over one of the big granite knobs he slipped and dislodged a mat of turf which revealed a long seam of white quartz threaded with little yellow veins. Bedford broke off a chunk and had it assayed. Yes, it was gold, so rich that a ton of it would be worth sixty thousand dollars.

Bedford hunted for that hill and that seam of quartz until he died but never found it again. One summer he even hired an experienced prospector from out west but he couldn't find it either. I know the tale is true because I held that heavy chunk in my own hands when my father took me to the station and while he played chess with Bedford. You could see the gold in it clearly. Dad said that chunk was probably worth more than a hundred dollars.

Then there was the tale told by Jim Olson, one of Dad's hunting cronies, who was the caretaker of the mining properties after the mines closed down. On the hills surrounding Silver Lake Jim had found an old iron door on a side slope that was so firmly fixed he could not budge it. Below that iron door in the swamp were chunks of blasted quartz, some of which had fine threads of gold in them.

And, of course, all of us knew of Old Man Coon, the hermit, who had spent thirty years putting shafts in the hills near the upper reaches of the Escanaba. I've been to his place and was impressed by the long piles of rock that he'd dug out of those shafts. Thirty years of hard, solitary labor. He must have found some gold.

So that is why, on a warm afternoon, I was roaming the hills with a frying pan and little prospector's pickaxe in my napsack. I'd panned for gold, swirling gravel around in the frying pan, in two little creeks but had found nothing. I'd found two seams of quartz next to greenstone that might possibly be promising and hacked out chunks that I could scrutinize later with a magnifying glass. I did find a fine sample of fool's gold, iron pyrites, with its little cubes of yellow. Absolutely worthless, of course. Always there was that dream of striking it rich. If I did, I wouldn't have to go Down Below to go to college and get a job and maybe never see my beloved U.P. again. I'd be another Old Man Coon, fishing, hunting and prospecting the rest of a wonderful life in the land I loved.

I came to a notch, a gulch, which I had to cross, and as I was working my way through it I heard water gurgling. Looking down I saw a little stream barely a foot wide flowing out of the earth below a fallen spruce. A spring! A spring! It had been a warm August day and I was perspiring, so I lay down to drink from a little pool. Waugh! It was no spring. The water was not ice cold but warm. I drank anyway but curious about its origin I walked up the gulch and found the stream again. What was the source? I had to know so I followed it upwards through a terrible tangle of alders and windfalls until suddenly I came out on the short of a narrow little lake.

A beautiful lake, it was, cradled in the granite hills, but what hit me immediately was the island. Right in the middle of the shimmering blue water was a narrow island with huge pines, virgin pines. Evidently the loggers who cut the pine in the old days had overlooked it. I could hardly wait to take off my clothes and swim the fifty yards to its shore, to a little sand and gravel beach. As I stood there dripping and naked, a strange feeling came over me, one that alas I cannot recapture. Sort of like Adam when he first entered the Garden of Eden, I suppose. I sat down on a log by the beach for a long time, then got up to explore. Actually there weren't many of those huge pines, perhaps only eight or ten of them, but they towered far into the sky. No underbrush, just a bed of pine needles so thick it was like walking on cushions. One old tree had fallen but beside it were several tiny pine saplings hunting for the sun.

I roamed the shoreline, most of which was covered by Labrador tea bushes or Michigan holly. The latter's berries were full formed but not as scarlet as they would be once frost came. The north shore was a great slab of granite and red feldspar which sloped then plunged into deep water. I ran down it and dived into the lake yelling Hallelujah, and felt ashamed because I'd broken its silence. Then I hugged one of those great pines, went back to the little beach, and swam to the other shore where my clothes were awaiting me. I remember hating to leave my island, wanting to stay there forever. I hadn't found any gold but I had found something infinitely better.

That was in 1926 and I revisited my little lake and island almost every year thereafter. Twice I slept overnight under the great pines, once completely naked, but covered by heaps of the brown needles. It wasn't good; the covering was too prickly though warm enough. The second time I floated over my clothes, a blanket, a coffee can and some food on a little raft, caught a trout and a perch, and spent the night on some moss just back from the beach. I remember that my little cooking fire seemed to desecrate the place and spoil the night so I put it out as soon as the fish were done, then cleaned up the site so that no one could ever know anyone had ever been there. Not that there was much chance of that.

Only once did I try to share my lake and island with another person, my newly wedded wife, Milove. She had heard me tell of my island sometimes at night when I held her in my arms but when we got to the base of the hills and she saw what she would have to go through to get to the lake she balked. I didn't blame her; indeed I felt relieved. Much as I loved my new bride I selfishly did not want her or anyone else to know my own secret place.

My island? It was not mine. It was owned by a big logging company as I discovered when I later tried to buy it and was refused. But in a larger sense I never felt that it was mine; rather that it possessed me. I was not an intruder; I was a part of that lovely island, as much a part as were those great pine trees. The moment I stepped ashore, dripping, it put its arms around me and I was safe, safe as being in Abraham's bosom.

Most of the people who have lived on an island tell me that they know that feeling well. They say that the water barrier creates a sense of sanctuary. Perhaps that's why castles had moats. Anyway, one of the vivid feelings I had on the island was that of complete safety. Not that I had any fears of wolves or bears; only those from Down Below fear them. Oh, we're leery when a bear has cubs and drives us away but that doesn't count. No, it's the safety from all evils, even from the personal demons that haunt all of us.

But there were other feelings too, some too deep to put into words. Up there on the island I felt cleansed both inside and out. After just a few hours there I always felt a sense of renewal, of new vigor, of potential for further growth. Hard to explain but the experience was vivid. Also there came an increased alertness. I saw things with strange eyes: three kinds of mosses and five varieties of ferns, to give but one example. My hearing seemed more acute: I actually heard two grasshoppers making love.

My sense of smell, long dormant due to pipe tobacco, awakened to fragrances and aromas I'd never known. One afternoon on the island I put my nose to everything I could find. Many of the scents were old friends but there were some new ones too. The best came from three white water lilies floating in a little bay by the point. No, I didn't pick them. There's nothing so sad as a wilted water lily - except perhaps the last drop of whiskey in the glass. Instead I joined them with just my floating face turned to the sun. Four water lilies! Some people claim that our wild white water lilies have no fragrance. They are wrong.

Then there was that delicious feeling of freedom. I could do any damned fool thing I wanted to do. No one could see or hear me or touch me - not even with their voices. No one could make demands. I had left all the pollution of civilization on the other side of many lovely hills. I felt primal, uncivilized, and beat my bare chest to assure myself that it was true. Drinking deeply of the solitude and isolation, that freedom almost intoxicated me.

But best of all was the feeling of peace, the peace that passeth understanding. All my little or big worries just vanished. Part of that was due to the deep quiet on my island. Oh, occasionally I became aware of the soft rustle of wind in the pine branches far above me, or the lapping of little waves on the shore, but these were murmurs, not noises. Lying there on a bed of moss with the sunshine on my face and body, all I heard was the utter silence. No one can describe that sort of peacefulness, but one of its elements seemed to be that time had stopped. No hurry, no urgency, no concern for what I should do next. That freedom from the tyranny of the clock that hassles our everyday lives was part of the peace I felt. But hell's bells, I'm almost talking like a preacher, a role that does not fit me.

Year after year I returned to my island, usually just once or twice, lest it lose its magical impact on me. It never did. Never was there any sign that any other human had been on its shores. Always I felt that same safety, cleansing, renewal, altertness, freedom and peace. Always I was reborn.

I missed going there only two years, once during World War II and once after I suffered my first heart attack. "Never get out of breath. Never over-exert," the doctors told me and getting to my island would have been too dangerous. A few years later, though, I started visiting my island again and kept it up annually until about nine years ago when more heart troubles and other betrayals of the flesh said no.

I have not seen it since. No, that is not true. I've seen it in the ambulance, in the hospital bed, at night here at home when I thought I might die. Always the vision has given me peace. At eighty-one I have no hope of ever going there again but that doesn't matter now. I had my island once and I have it still. May you find an island of your own.

A MARRIAGE OF CONVENIENCE

When John Sivola came into the house after feeding and watering his horses he swore. The coffee had boiled over on the wood range and the bacon was burned again. Another lousy breakfast! He'd had a lot of them as well as other bad meals ever since his wife Siiri had died.

Stirring an egg into the charred bacon and straining the coffee through a square of window screen into a dirty cup John ate the mess right out of the frying pan. No way to live, he thought. A man needed a woman.

He looked around the house. It was a fine house, a frame house, not a log cabin. He had built it with his own hands for Siiri but oh it was so dirty now. The hardwood floors that she had kept scrubbed until they shone had barn dirt ground into them because he forgot to put on the barn boots when he took care of the horses. Siiri never let him forget. And the windows were so dirty it was hard to see out of them. And all those dishes piled in the sink. It would take an

hour to clean them and then they'd soon be dirty again. He thought of the bedroom with the bed that hadn't been made for months and the pile of dirty sheets and blankets in the corner. He'd done a washing several times, a long nasty job, and tried some ironing as the big brown spot on one of the sheets testified. And his own clothes were so bad he hated to put them on in the morning. He needed a woman to take care of those things.

As he fixed a ham sandwich for his lunch in the woods where he was cutting pulp off one of the three forties he owned John hated the store bread that he smeared with mustard. Weak stuff if was. Siiri's homemade bread had always clung to the ribs and made him feel full. No, he wasn't eating right and he knew it. Too much bacon, pork and beans, and bologna and store soup. It wasn't that he lacked for money. No, he had plenty of raha in the bank but he hated to go to Flynn's store for groceries. Siiri had always done the shopping. When he did go now he always forgot something and had to go back again and again. The cellar shelves, once filled with canned venison and berries and applesauce, were empty now and in the summer there always were fresh vegetables from the garden she tended. John had planted a garden last year after she died but got little from it because of the weeds. The kitchen no longer had that fine smell of cinnamon rolls or pies baking in the oven. Indeed it smelled faintly of horse manure. "And so do I", he said to himself. It had been fun to go sauna with Siiri; not much fun to go alone. Something had to be done. He couldn't keep on living this way.

John took a big wad of Peerless and put it in his pipe. It was time to do some hard thinking, and the first thought was that he'd have to get married again. Filled with guilt, he rejected it at first. This was Siiri's house. How could he bear to have another woman in it? A flood of memories of her returned but again and again it became clear that he could no longer live alone. He would have to find another wife.

But who? At sixty-three years of age, no young girl would look at him and besides he didn't think he could handle the sex business if he did find one. No, the best bet would be a widow. There were three of them in town, Aunt Lizzie, hell no!, and Mrs. Belanger but she was French Canadian and Catholic and that was out. The third was Helmi Heikkenen whose husband had been killed two years before when a beam fell on him in the railroad roundhouse. John didn't know her very well. He'd seen her at church before he stopped going there. A plump woman, fairly good looking, and easy to talk to, she lived in a log cabin up by Sliding Rock. A real possibility. Maybe she needed a man as much as he needed a woman.

But how to go about courting her? How to find out if she might be interested? It had been easy with Siiri. He'd carried her books home from high school and they had walked many miles down the railroad tracks after church talking up a storm. John didn't know how it came about but suddenly they were married. Eighteen she was, and he nineteen. They'd lived together happily until the scarlet fever killed her. John knew that he couldn't just up and tell Helmi Heikkenen that he needed a wife to do the cleaning and washing and cooking. No, he would have to court her. But how? There was nothing to do in Tioga, no place to go except to church. Each evening at nine the kerosene lamps of the village winked out except for those in Higley's saloon and the railroad station. Maybe, after they got acquainted, he could hitch up one of his draft horses to the buckboard and go for a ride down to Lake Tioga some afternoon if she were willing. Yes, getting acquainted was the first step.

So John Sivola shaved, put on the cleanest shirt, and drove his team and lumber wagon up to Flynn's store, bought some hamburger and a chicken and some cookies, then took the back road home past Helmi's log cabin hoping to see her in the yard. She wasn't but John noticed that the smoke coming out of her chimney was not emerging from its top but rather from its base where the bricks joined the roof. That's a dangerous business so John knocked on the cabin door. When Helmi opened it he told her what he had seen.

"Helmi, going by I see smoke coming out at bottom of your chimney. You could have bad fire that way. You want me to fix it?"

She thanked him warmly for his concern but said that she had no money to pay him. John smiled. "Oh, that's OK" he said. "I do it for free. I got bricks and cement at home. I go get them. But can I come in to see if bottom of chimney is bad too?"

The cabin was spotless, the windows sparkling clean, and there were good cooking smells. Helmi's hands were floured from bread making. "I give you cup of coffee, John," she said, "but coffee is all gone until next week when pension check comes. You want some maitua (milk)? I got lots of milk now that my cow just freshened and eggs and butter and soon have fresh bread. I give you new bread with butter and wild strawberry jam when you come back." John could tell that she was feeling bad that she couldn't offer coffee. In the U.P. you always "give coffee" when someone drops in.

John returned that afternoon with the wagon filled with bricks, a mixing box, sand and cement. The cement and bricks were left over from the outhouse he'd built for Siiri when she got tired of the boys dumping it over every Halloween; the sand he got from the beach at Lake Tioga. The job took him all afternoon but it was done right and Helmi sure appreciated it. As they sat across the kitchen table afterward eating fresh bread smeared heavily with butter and wild strawberry jam she told him so.

"It's hard without a man in the house," she said. "Most things I can do but big things no. Hard for you too, John, I think, now that Siiri is gone. I do washing tomorrow and if you bring me basket of your dirty clothes I wash them for you, eh? We help each other." Though sorely tempted, John refused her offer. "My clothes too dirty." As he left, she gave him a piece of blueberry pie for his supper.

The next day he had to work in the woods and there was plenty of time to think. Yah, they would hit it off. Yah, she needed him as he needed her. How soon should he wait before asking her? Being acquainted only one day not long enough. Was he ready yet to go to bed with another woman? No! Would he ever be? Maybe so, but not yet. Meanwhile he should try to see her often. Her cabin needed new wood plaster chinking; a bottom log was rotten and needed replacing; her barn and chicken coop were in bad shape. No point to fixing up those because he'd have to build some new ones for her when she moved into his house. But to have some excuse for seeing her now, he'd fix that bottom log and do the chinking. John cut down a fine cedar that he could use.

The second day of his courting John brought her a pail of coffee beans and when he found that her coffee grinder was broken and she was tring to grind them with a hammer in a dish, he repaired it. All it needed was a shim around the axle of the little cog wheel. Taking most of the afternoon to replace the rotten log and chink the other logs, he was rewarded by a fine supper of maijuka (venison stew), Helmi having found in her cellar one last jar of the canned deer meat. And coffee and applesauce for dessert. Sitting there across from her at the red checkered table cloth, John felt not only full but more at peace than he had been for many months. Twice he almost broached the subject of marriage but it seemed too soon. Instead he asked her if she would be willing to come see his house the next day and show him how to wash his sheets. No matter how hard he boiled them, they were always grey.

"Did you put bleach or blueing in the wash water?" Helmi asked.

"No. I don't know if I have them," he replied. "I use plenty of soap though. I buy some if you show me. And kituksia (thanks) for the fine meal. I sure love your leipa (bread)." Helmi agreed.

So the next afternoon he came for her after cleaning up his house and washing the dishes and making the bed. The sheets were still hanging out on the line and he had the copper boiler steaming on the stove. Helmi brought in the sheets, poured some of the bleach and blueing she had brought with her into the boiler, put in the sheets and then went with him all over the house and to his barn and even to his pasture and hayfields. Then she rinsed and put the sheets through the wringer and hung them on the clothesline outside, singing as she did so. Soon they were white-white and despite his protests, she ironed them in his kitchen, folded them and placed them on his bed. Before she left she also cleaned his sink, using some of the bleach. John was overwhelmed. "Oh, kituskia (thanks) Helmi," he said. "You good woman. Now I know how to do it."

But he hoped he wouldn't ever have to do it again.

The next day, lacking anything else he could do to help her, John split a lot of firewood and kindling. When he came in for coffee and coffeecake, he finally popped the question.

"Helmi, will you marry me" he said. "You and I have hard time living lone. We need each other. You poor. I have lots of raha in the bank. I make good money and give you all you need. I need someone to cook for me, and wash, and clean. I lonesome and maybe you are too. Only bad thing is that I don't want any love stuff. Too close to Siiri yet." Helmi lifted an eyebrow at that and said that she'd think it over.

The next day when he brought her a box of chocolates from Flynn's store she gave John her answer and with it a bombshell. Yes, she would marry him. It was a business bargain with no love stuff as he had made clear. But she wouldn't move into his house; she would stay right here in her own. He could eat his meals here and she would pack his lunch pail. She would do his washing when he brought it to her, and once each week she would go to his house to clean it up. He would give her money for food or anything else she wanted to buy. He would do chores for her like splitting wood and kindling. She would feed him good. But she was staying in her own cabin not moving into his house. No love stuff. He would sleep in his own bed, not in hers. A business bargain.

Well, that sure surprised John Sivola so much his mouth hung open. Yet it made sense. The people in town would do a lot of tongue wagging once they found out but nuts to them. When Helmi brought out some coffee and hot cinnamon rolls it took only one bit to convince him. "Yah," he said. "Tomorrow we take afternoon train to Ishpeming and get married by Justice of Peace."

So that is what they did. John got two copies of the marriage license, one for him and one for her, and had them framed in a little shop next door. Then he insisted on buying her a new dress and shoes and a bright new huivi (head scarf) with lace on it before he took her to the Chocolate Shop for the biggest banana split they had. That was their honeymoon.

When they got off the evening train and walked up our long hill street, John leading the way and Helmi following, as was the custom for married but not unmarried Finns, they met Aunt Lizzie on her gossip rounds. "Helmi, you and John get married?" she asked. "I see that he fixed your house and they say that you went to Ishpeming to get married."

John stepped in. "Yah, we get married though none of your business. I marry fine woman." By the time they climbed the hill and were at Helmi's house, the whole town knew. And approved. Two nice people should not live alone.

When they got there Helmi told John to go to his house to feed and water his horses while she fixed his supper. Before he left, however, he put her copy of the marriage certificate on the shelf above the kitchen stove and left under the coffee grinder a wad of green money. "This for you, Helmi," he said, "and you can have all you want anytime." It was an awkward moment, almost as though he was buying a wife, but she smiled on him as he left. He liked that smile. Things would work out.

When John returned, they had supper. Not much of a wedding feast but very good. The rest of the venison stew and a piece of yesterday's pie and some more cinnamon rolls. Helmi apologized. "I make you good meal tomorrow, John, after I go store."

Smoking his pipe afterwards, he heard her singing softly as she did the dishes. Was it the Finn Marrying Song? No, it was Kuopia, a song about a lonesome wanderer who had finally come home. "Miksi tau tu sineh o Lempia, miksi tau tu raukusta." His mother had sung it to him when he was a child. John lit pipe after pipe, hating to go home to an empty house. So warm, so full fed and happy he was he could hardly bear to leave. Ah, she was a fine woman, Helmi was, and a happy woman. So he dallied.

It was a good thing that he did for suddenly outside there came a hullabaloo of yelling and the banging on pans. "Oh, oh," Helmi cried, "They give us chivari, I think. How they find out so soon?"

"We let them make noise for a while, then I pay them." John responded.

Finally came the knocks on the door and shouts of "Chivari, Chivari!" John went out to confront the twenty young men and boys. "We go to your house first," one of them said, "but you no there. We find you anyway. Pay!" John grinned. "OK," he replied. "Here four bucks, three for your keg of beer and one for boys' candy. You go away now and leave us alone." When they departed, John said to Helmi, "Well I guess we married now, eh? And I must go my house. I don't want to go." He looked at her but saw no sign of protest. "Good night, John," she said, "I have breakfast for you at seven."

It was a short winter for the U.P. that year with ice out by the end of March. John shot a deer much of which Helmi canned and many rabbits and partridge so they ate well. He also shot two geese which Helmi plucked, using the down to make him a pillow for his bed. "So you will think of me" she said. Think of her? She was always in his thoughts.

As the winter wore on, the business bargain arrangement began to seem not right to John. Almost always the fire was out in the stove when he returned to his empty house each night. He got tired of having to bring her his clothes to

121

wash. It was hard too for Helmi to go to his house each week to keep it clean, having to go down our long hill street, then up Keystone Hill, then back again. John usually came to her house the back way on his skis and so feeling sorry for her, he brought over Siiri's old skis so she could do the same. Made him feel guilty but not too much. Helmi was a good skier and once the two of them skied cross-country over to Big Rock on Fish Lake and had a pot of coffee over a campfire just as though they were courting.

Only once in that long time did Helmi show him some real affection. He had brought her a perfect little spruce Christmas tree one morning before going to the woods and when he returned she had it all decorated with colored chains of paper, and popcorn strung on threads, yes, even with a bright star on top that she had painfully cut from the top of a tin can. Sure looked pretty and when he told her so and said that she did too she patted his check. That was all but he felt her soft hand for weeks.

Yet once, when impulsively he swept her onto his lap, she fought back like a wild cat, hitting and slashing him till he let her go. And didn't cook a bite for him for a day. "Don't you forget. Business-bargain, business-bargain, no love stuff," she shouted. John went back to his house early that night.

But spring came, the miraculously lovely U.P. spring. The snow melted and, hoping one day that Helmi might too, John brought her a great armful of blue flags (wild iris) from a swamp that had soaked him over his knees. She was overcome with delight and showed it.

"Why you bring me flowers, John?" she asked.

He swallowed twice, then said, "Because I love you, Helmi."

She cupped a hand to her ear. "Say again!" she ordered. "and again and again!" Then Helmi put her arms around his neck and kissed him. "Oh Johnny, why you no say that before?" But after supper she insisted again that he go back to his own house.

As he lay there with his head on the goosedown pillow John wondered about the inscrutable ways of women. Why did she send him home? Maybe spring thaw had come to her but deep ice doesn't melt all at once. Remembering her bare arms around his neck, he slept deeply.

The next morning all was the same except that Helmi had made blueberry pancakes with store sausage and had put a hot pasty in his dinner pail. As they ate across from each other the blue flags in a big bowl separated yet joined them and when he left for the woods she patted his cheek again. Yes, the ice was melting.

That afternoon as he returned from cutting spruce John drove his team to Flynn's store to pick up another box of chocolates but when he entered Helmi's house she was not there. Probably having coffee with the neighbors. Too early for supper yet, so he drove the team to his barn, fed and watered it, then entered his house to wash up. Helmi met him at the door. "Oh, Johnny," she exclaimed as she put her arms around his neck. "Meet Helmi Sivola, your new bride. This is my house too now. I move in to stay." There was meat cooking on the stove and the blue flags were on the kitchen table so John said it again. "I love you, Helmi." And they lived happily ever after.

ANDREW AMOR, Illustrator

Andy Amor, Architect, Woodcarver, Artist, and Musician, has brought his vivid feelings and conceptions to this series of impressions by Cully Gage. "My perception of the U.P. has certainly been tainted with Cully Gage's folklore. I asked him if this view was true or was based on mere fiction". He replied as his Grandpa Gage once did, "Should it be true?!!"

It is with this spirit that Andy Amor illustrated these stories, to make each drawing authentically believable and at the same time unbelievably true.

Andrew Amor lives with his wife Elizabeth (Cully's granddaughter), in Ann Arbor, Michigan, and enjoys summer trips to the U.P. wilds with Cully.

PLEASE RETURN TO:

Avery **Color Studios**
Star Route - Box 275
Au Train, Michigan 49806
Phone: (906) 892-8251
IN MICHIGAN
CALL TOLL FREE
1-800-722-9925

Your complete shipping address:

_____

_____

_____

Fold, Staple, Affix Stamp and Mail

Avery COLOR STUDIOS
Star Route - Box 275
AuTrain, Michigan 49806